the road to glory

by josh heupel

The Road to Glory

Josh Heupel with Bob Schaller, The Road to Glory

ISBN 1-929478-25-9

Cross Training Publishing
317 West Second Street
Grand Island, NE 68801
(308) 384-5762

Published by Cross Training Publishing,
317 West Second Street
Grand Island, NE 68801

Photo Credits: © Jerry Laizure, pages: 1, 12-16, and cover. Other photographs provided courtesy of Cindy Heupel

A portion of the proceeds from this book support the following organizations:

The #14 Foundation

Mission Statement:
The #14 Foundation will make a difference in the lives of people. Faith is the number one priority in determining the course of our foundation. Through faith we will lead, unite, and inspire others to honor all people.

"The #14 Foundation is something that allows me to help young people in a tangible way. I can have a positive impact on children and youth and provide them with opportunities for a more fulfilling life." Josh Heupel

The Fellowship of Christian Athletes

Purpose:
To present to athletes and coaches, and all whom they influence, the challenge and adventure of receiving Jesus Christ as their Savior and Lord, serving Him in their relationships and in the fellowship of the church.

To contact either the #14 Foundation or the Fellowship of Christian Athletes in Oklahoma:

Mike Whitson
P.O. Box 1613
Norman, OK 73070
(405) 366-6485

#14 Foundation
P.O. Box 912
Aberdeen, SD 57401

PREFACE BY
JOSH HEUPEL

The format of this book is unique. What I tried to do with co-author Bob Schaller is present my story from my faith to the lessons I've learned through pursuing goals.

The first part of the book is third-person with background provided by family, friends and coaches.

In the second part of the book you will read about my feelings and thoughts on the unlikely path of faith that took me from Aberdeen, South Dakota, to Utah and then to Oklahoma and points beyond.

In the final part of this book, you will read the 2000 National Championship season for the University of Oklahoma. We included boxscores and game notes to each of the games. And finally, we have provided the play by play for the Big 12 Championship Game against Kansas State and the Orange Bowl against Florida State for the National Championship.

I hope you enjoy the journey because that's the most important part.

INTRODUCTION BY BARRY SWITZER
FORMER OKLAHOMA SOONERS,
HEAD FOOTBALL COACH

There is no doubt that Josh Heupel left Sooner fans with a lot of memories on the field.

But what he left off the field will be remembered the most. It will be remembered the longest, and for all the right reasons.

Josh is a true role model. Through his actions he demonstrated the kind of person he is. Yet he did that without having to say a word because of how he carries himself. He is not flamboyant. There are those who speak out and proclaim their faith—people who are very boisterous about who they are—but it can be for self-image and other reasons. Josh has never been that way. It's always been obvious how impressive Josh's character is without saying anything. He truly is as perfect a role model as you will find.

Kids he comes in contact with and the guys on his team want to emulate him, and Josh doesn't have to say a word. He always leads by example.

Taking a moment to think about it, really, it is amazing. The program won a national championship in 2000, in just the second year at OU for head coach Bob Stoops, after the program had endured several rough years before Coach Stoops took over.

Oklahoma always has recruited good players. Under Coach Stoops they orchestrated those players and had everything in place to execute the game plan. Every team that has this kind of success has to have good players, but they have to have a great leader.

There is no doubt in my mind—as a coach and someone who observed this program—that the re-emergence of this program, complete with reaching the national pinnacle, would not have happened without Josh.

He was the right person at the right time in the history of this program. No one else could have gotten them back to the top as quickly as Josh Heupel.

People have asked me how Josh fits in with the great quarterbacks of all-time at Oklahoma. But the system the player is in has to be considered. So who is the best? I don't know if there's an answer for that question. But I can tell you that Josh coming into this system was the perfect fit. He has intelligence, poise and a knowledge of the game that is unbelievable. His perception and his vision on the field are second to none. Josh has all the intangibles a coach—at any level, from Pop Warner to the NFL—is looking for in a quarterback.

So when OU was in a hurry to put together a national championship caliber team very quickly under Coach Stoops, they had to have a quarterback who had all of those qualities. There could not have been a better quarterback for what Coach Stoops and his staff were trying to accomplish than Josh Heupel.

The fact that he came here as a junior is a tough break for OU fans. In fact, having him here only two years is a shame. Josh accomplished more in two years than most college football players do at their respective colleges in four and five years.

But the kind of impact Josh had will never be forgotten.

FOREWORD BY BOB STOOPS
OKLAHOMA SOONERS, HEAD FOOTBALL COACH

Though Josh Heupel is serious and takes care of business, he has a very good nature about himself.

All of our players loved him, and loved being around him. He doesn't segregate the players, or people for that matter, by rich or poor, by race or ethnic background, or by age or religion. He made it a point to make all those around him know that they mattered to him. That is why he's a good leader.

We first recruited Josh back in early 1999. My offensive coordinator at the time, Mike Leach, had known of Josh while Josh was at Snow College in Utah. Mike showed me some tape on Josh, and I liked him as well. I liked the way Josh played the game, his poise, his accuracy, and his ability to make the right reads. He was very bright.

And, of course, he won; we really liked that about him as we recruited him.

When he arrived for his recruiting visit, he knew all about the academic excellence at the University of Oklahoma. He just wanted to see the direction the football program was moving in as we put together our first preseason plans for the upcoming 1999 season. All Josh wanted to do was watch tape with Mike Leach. They would go for virtually four or five hours at a time just watching tape.

I think what Josh wanted to do was make sure that he could help this team and that we had the kind of offense he could be successful in. His attitude was, "Yes, I can do this."

He figured we already had the athletes at Oklahoma to get this done. What Josh was looking for was the best chance to win. He had one primary question for me when he and I spoke on campus while we recruited him.

"I just want to know, can we win a conference and national championship here in my first two years?" Josh asked me.

"With you here, I think we can," I told him. Everything else was in place, and a few other things had to develop. But Josh being worried only about winning championships tells you a lot about who he is. He knew he couldn't do it alone, so he wanted to know about the team and the entire program. I was impressed that Josh already realized the importance—and necessity—of teamwork.

The film work and his commitment to working out and being a leader in our off-season programs is why Josh is such a great leader. He leads by example, by the way he prepares, and the way he's worked himself into being a great player. He has talent, but he's reached the level he's at with hard work. And as you saw in 2000, his toughness is just exceptional.

Josh's sense of humility is one of the things I remember most. He always set the tone that no matter how much success an individual player has, the team is more important. He set a great example for our players for the future.

He finished just behind Chris Weinke of Florida State in the Heisman Trophy voting. It would have been nice if Josh had received the Heisman—in fact, that would have been great.

If Josh had to choose between the Heisman Trophy and the National Championship Trophy, there is no doubt he would have chosen the national championship. And that's the one we won. So Josh got the trophy he truly coveted. Being carried off the field at the Orange Bowl after beating Florida State for the national championship is something Josh will remember forever.

And so will I.

Bob Stoops

CONTENTS

1

Daring Delivery

The snow was blowing badly, a whipping wind swirling fresh powder along the South Dakota-North Dakota border, not uncommon in the winter months and early spring.

Cindy and Ken Heupel were at the hospital in Aberdeen, awaiting the birth of their first child on March 22, 1978.

When Joshua Kenneth Heupel entered the world that evening, the snow was still falling. Three days later when it was time for Ken and Cindy to take their new baby home, nine miles south of the North Dakota border.

The owners of the farm and the house in which Ken and Cindy lived were Ken's parents, Theophil and Bertha Heupel, who lived in the North Dakota border town of Ashley, though Ken and Cindy's home on the farm was within the South Dakota border.

But getting home that Easter Sunday afternoon wasn't easy. The near whiteout conditions were making the last leg on the drive—a small blacktop State Highway 45—treacherous. When they got within less than a half mile of the farmhouse, Ken called ahead.

A snowmobile met the family at the entrance to the property, and with the little boy wrapped in blankets and a parka, the last leg of the trip was completed to the small two-story house.

The only problem was that high drifts of snow had made the front door almost invisible. So Ken walked the baby one-quarter of a mile as Cindy rode on the snowmobile.

Josh wasn't a sickly little boy, but a series of ear infections and the croup kept him in and out of the hospital until he was four.

"Josh never complained when he was sick," said Cindy. "He was so good-natured that we had no idea he was sick until the condition became acute."

Cindy's sister, Julie, had moved in with them when Josh was a baby. And Josh liked having his aunt Julie living with him.

"He was six months old, and he'd sit on the counter as we made gingerbread cookies together," Julie said. "His little shirt would be off, and his diaper would be full of flour from 'helping' me make gingerbread cookies."

Josh continued to get sick off and on. But each time, the doctor would pronounce Josh fit, and the family would be on its way.

"His motor skills are advanced," the family doctor told Josh's parents. "He's a very healthy young man. Just try to keep up with him."

Cindy worried when Josh was a baby because sometimes his hands would shake. They went to the University of Minnesota Medical Center.

"His doctors said he was fine, that he was just trying to do things that wouldn't happen until later on the growth chart," Cindy said. "He was always pushing his physical limits. He was always exploring—very kinesthetic."

At about eight months, Josh started walking.

"And by 10 months," his mother said, "he was running."

The family moved to a rented house in Aberdeen, on Eisenhower Circle, when Josh was six months old. When he was two, the parents moved into a ranch-style, three-bedroom house in one of the newer areas of Aberdeen, on Apollo Avenue.

Josh had a picture of an elephant on the ceiling above his crib.

"He was very alert," Cindy said, "and into shapes and colors and studying everything."

As a baby, Josh loved playing with any kind of ball. He had 102 balls—the family counted—when he was two years old.

"Tennis balls, footballs, baseballs—even racquetballs," Cindy said. "That's all he ever wanted. If you bought him a ball, he'd play with it."

When Cindy's younger sister, Julie, was living with Ken and Cindy, Josh was just nine months old. She started dating the man who eventually would become her husband, Pat. Josh took a liking to Pat. About five months into dating, Pat came over to take Julie to a movie.

"The kid always had a ball in his hand," Pat said. "I don't ever remember going over there and not seeing Josh with a ball."

Especially the night of the movie.

"I got there for our date about 6 p.m., because the movie would start at 7 p.m.," Pat recalls. "I always liked to leave a little time to play with Josh. Well, he was 14 months old by then, and he came walking out and making these noises—he didn't really talk yet, but he knew exactly what he wanted. And that was to play catch. He walks over to his toy box, and gets this catcher's mask that, at the time, had to be about 20 years old, this hard iron thing with thick leather pads around it. He motioned for me to put it on, and we started playing catch. It gets to be about 6:30, so I stood to take off the mask, and Josh just throws a fit. 'OK, it's OK, bud, we'll play a little more, and we'll just cut it a little close making it to the movie.'

I'm starting to sweat pretty badly because of that mask. We ended up playing for four hours. Cindy and Julie ended up going to the show together. In fact, they got home from the movie, and we were still playing. We stopped at 10 p.m. because he needed a new diaper and his dad swept him off to bed."

Josh was very attached to Julie. At night, he'd always try to extend his bedtime. Julie would compromise.

"He wanted to come in and sleep in my bed," Julie said. "He was so cute. So I usually gave in."

Julie remembers those days fondly.

"A pacifier, a ball—he'd throw anything," Julie said. "There was always a motivation or goal; he didn't want to throw it. He wanted to hit something with it."

And that explains the cartoon that was given to Cindy. A friend of hers found the cartoon in a magazine at a doctor's office and was so sure Cindy needed it that she tore it out. There's a little boy in a chair at a dinner table with a football helmet on.

"A mother is serving food and the parents look haggard. The caption has the mother saying to the husband, 'Whatever you do, don't ask him to pass anything.' That's the way it was with Josh," Cindy said.

Literally.

2

That Kid and His Arm

The propensity to throw things was never more evident than when Josh was two. His family went out to Southwestern Oregon to visit his grandparents, Gladys and Thomas Kelly. Cindy and Ken went out to dinner, so the grandparents watched Josh. His grandfather gave him a rubber ball as Josh sat in his training pants in front of the fireplace. Far above the fireplace on a high mantle was a statue of St. Francis.

"Josh went to the other side of the room and started throwing the ball, bouncing it off the area above the fireplace," Gladys said. "He was pitching it, raising his little leg like the baseball pitchers do on TV. Grandpa and I were clapping because he was doing so well, throwing it and then running around pretend bases each time. Well, he kept throwing it higher and higher, so we clapped more and more. And then …"

And then Josh threw it higher yet, catching St. Francis, who, of course, wasn't wearing a mitt.

"St. Francis was beheaded that night—and it crashed to the floor," Gladys said. "It never dawned on us while we watched, but that was what he was aiming for the entire time, throwing it higher and higher. It was a pretty sentimental statue to us, and we'd had it for quite a while. The poor little guy had no idea, though. After we reacted and picked it up, Josh picked up his ball and threw it the other way, saying, 'Bad ball!' for breaking the statue."

Also when he was two years old, Josh would run routes in the front yard with his father, and his Uncle Wil Heupel who was calling the plays.

In the house, Uncle Wil Heupel had bought Josh a blow-up Pittsburgh Steelers doll.

"At nine months, Josh was tackling that thing," Cindy said. "Wil was a Steelers fan. We'd get him a Vikings jacket, and Wil would get him a Steelers sweatshirt."

While writing his masters thesis in the fall of 1980, Uncle Wil lived with Josh's family.

"I would look at how much that kid was eating, we thought he'd be a lineman or a linebacker," Wil said. "You couldn't put enough food down that boy."

At age two, Josh's parents bought him a Nerf basketball hoop for his birthday. Josh would make his mother play with him every night.

"He was into anything and everything that had to do with sports," Cindy said.

Everything, that is, except sleep.

"He didn't sleep through the night until he was two and a half years old," Cindy says. "He wasn't crabby or anything; he just wanted to visit. I finally took him to the doctor and told him, 'Josh is always hungry, and he never sleeps!' The doctor said, 'He's just fine.' Well, he finally slept through the night. And I remember waking up that morning—the first time we had slept through the night in about 30 months— and my first thought was, 'Oh, no, my baby is dead!' I went running into his room, and there he was sleeping soundly. Finally."

According to Cindy's other sister, Charlotte Anderson, Josh could turn a simple shopping trip into a competition. It is on those shopping trips he honed his quarterback sneak and scrambling skills.

"I used to take him shopping, and he'd hide in the clothes rack," Char said. "That was bad because he saw it as a competition to find him. And when he competed like that he was a pain, because he wanted to win, even back then. Shopping was not one of those things we did with Josh very often. It was all a big game."

At home in the yard, Char received her first introduction to football.

"He was three years old, and he wanted me to throw the football to him," Char said. "He was getting frustrated, and I was like, 'What, Josh?' He was diagramming plays he wanted me to do with him. I couldn't believe it."

When he was four, his grandma, Gladys Kelly, was visiting and decided to teach Josh how to tell time.

"Let's work on it tomorrow, Grandma," Josh said.

Gladys gave him a one-day reprieve. Then, on Monday, they went to the library in Aberdeen. Josh knew exactly where to go, having been there several times.

"He went right to the sports section," Gladys said. "He checked out some books on baseball, hockey, football and even one on swimming."

Inside the cover on the football book was a diagram of a football field, complete with marked yard lines and end zones, with the yards measured off in fives and tens just like on a regular football field.

Grandma took a box of Popsicle sticks, a box of toothpicks and a roll of twine and gave it to Josh. He made a football field, copying it out of the book.

"That's how he learned his fives and tens that day," Gladys said, "and that's how he learned to tell time."

Later in the day, Josh did that one better. He went into his parents' room and emptied out the bottom drawer in his mother's dresser. He drew a football field with a green marker and a black marker.

Also when he was four, the croup grabbed hold of Josh.

"Josh and I spent many nights in the bathroom with the shower running for steam. I slept on the floor with him," Cindy said. "There was one night I sat straight up in bed because the noise was so bad. It sounded like there was a seal in the house. We took him to the emergency room, and he spent five days in the hospital."

His parents knew Josh wanted a younger sibling. Ken and Cindy wanted to adopt a South-American baby. However, Cindy became pregnant, and on May 19, 1982, Andrea Heupel was welcomed into the world.

Josh was waiting at home, eager to see his little sister.

"He was really, really ready for a sibling," Cindy said. "He was so excited. He had always been asking us for a brother or sister. He was so excited to have a sister. He treated her like royalty. He was absolutely doting. He entertained her all the time and took very good care of her. She didn't walk until 15 months—she didn't have to because whenever she needed anything, Josh would do it. Andrea was a perfectionist, so she didn't want to do anything until she could do it perfectly. She just laughed and laughed at Josh all of the time because his main goal in life was to entertain her. And as she grew older, she always thought her mission in life was to help her brother."

As many will point out, Josh is competitive and will do whatever it takes to win. However, there's one game he'll never win.

"We always played checkers, and he never beat me," Grandma Gladys said. "I think that got to him a little when he was younger. Of course, I could still beat him. Then again, he probably wouldn't challenge me."

Josh decided he wanted to learn to skate at age four. So, on a frozen pond, he braved the elements.

"They put a red snow suit on him, and we went out to the pond," Grandma Gladys said. "Ken, Cindy, Tom and I went out there, and Josh thought he had to learn it all the first night. He was that determined. We were out there for a long time. It was getting dark, and we told Josh it was time to go home. Josh said, 'No, no, I'm not done.' We finally got him home and took his skates off, and his little feet were full of blisters. He was just so determined to learn to skate that he wasn't even thinking about that at the time."

His preschool care provider, Norma Frederickson, was married to a football coach, so Josh warmed up to her quickly. When Josh would head to Norma's for preschool, everyone in the neighborhood knew what time it was each day.

"All of the kids would get there, and they'd get on those three-wheeled things—the Big Wheels—right away, and head down the street," Grandma Gladys said. "They'd head down the sidewalk in the summer, and you'd hear the windows on the houses down the line closing like dominoes as the kids went past the house—from the noise of the Big Wheels."

Grandma Bertha remembers when her son, Ken, got the coaching job at Aberdeen Central. She and Grandpa Theophil went down to the school, with Ken giving them a tour. Grandson Josh went along. Everyone was amazed when they got to the locker room.

"Josh went over to the chalkboard," Grandma Bertha recalls, "and started drawing a game plan with X's and O's. That was just unbelievable. That was his interest, though—it just started at a young age. Being around his father's team at Central and then at Northern State really exposed him to that kind of thing at a young age and I think really encouraged the development of his interest in football."

When Josh got to kindergarten, he didn't know what to expect.

"When he walked into his kindergarten classroom, he immediately noticed that his teacher must have liked the Minnesota Vikings because she had a pennant on the wall," Cindy said. "So when we were shopping near Christmas time at the Mall in Minneapolis, Josh got a coffee cup for Mrs. White because he knew she liked the Vikings."

Like most kids, Josh loved watching TV. Unlike most kids, Josh didn't focus on cartoons or other kids shows. He watched sports, dissecting the games. He was so insistent upon having sports on TV that his father got him a small television at age four.

"We were watching every sports event that there could be," Ken said. "We were watching bowling. Who watches bowling? We did. He was four years old. We got him a TV and headphones that plugged into it. He'd sit there in his little chair in the corner of the living room."

The first night was the last for that first TV.

"The Minnesota North Stars were on," Ken recalls. "He had the headphones on. About 10 minutes into the game, Minnesota scored. Josh yells, 'And Dino Ciccarelli scores!' He jumped up and ran out to tell us. But he never took off the headphones. That TV came crashing down."

Josh was ready for team sports at age four. However, the hockey league accepted kids who were at least five years old.

"I was working with gifted education at the time, which involved getting gifted kids the opportunity to do things before the chronological age chart said it should be," Cindy said. "So we were trying to find outlets that welcomed that, which can be frustrating. I knew that socially, Josh was ready to develop and move along—that he was ready for those things."

So Josh played hockey and baseball. He'd also be in swimming lessons in addition to pursuing what would be his two favorite sports, football and basketball.

"Josh has always had a passion for athletics—of course, he's quite a passionate person," Cindy said. "But he was never in it for himself. He's such a leader."

While a lot of kids were playing with various toys, video games and even computers, Josh's true—and only—love was sports.

"He was a student of any game he played," Ken said. "He just loved athletics. He'd be watching golf, bowling, pool, anything that dealt with sports. You can't force kids to do anything. They pick it up and go with what makes them happy. Sports were the one that made him happy. He didn't really like trucks or computers or anything else."

When Josh was six years old, his father's team had a big game against the state's top ranked team, Mitchell, at Aberdeen's field. Central was not ranked.

"We were playing them real well early," Ken said. "Probably three minutes into the third quarter, we had fourth and inches."

Central was on its own 45-yard line. It was a risky call. Ken called a play-action pass. The receiver was wide open. However, so was a Mitchell linebacker, and that's where the errant pass went.

"The linebacker took it in for a TD," Ken said. "And from there, we ended up losing it, big. That was the turning point in the game. Things just snowballed from there."

After he and Josh put away the equipment, a common routine after games, home or away, they got into the car to head home.

Ken was deep in thought about what went wrong.

So was Josh.

"Dad, who is the offensive coordinator?" Josh asked.

"Well, I am," Ken said.

There was a pause.

"So then, Dad, who called that fourth and one play-action?" Josh asked.

"Well, I did," Ken answered.

"Dad," Josh said, "that's the dumbest call I've ever seen in my life. We should have punted. We were playing good defense."

Ken was caught off guard.

"You know, Josh was right," Ken recalls. "Momentum changed quickly, and that was the turning point of the game."

When Josh turned seven years old, the critiques became more detailed.

Father and son were driving home from the school after suffering a loss to O-Gorman, a private school in Sioux Falls. But this wasn't just any loss. This was a season-ender. The most painful of losses to the competitive ones. Had Ken's Central team won that semifinal game, they would have made the state championship game.

"That was the coldest game I can remember," Ken says. "With the wind chill, it was 30 below zero. We had heaters on the sidelines, straw on the grounds—the whole works."

Josh and his father were heading back from Aberdeen Central, where they had put away the team's equipment.

Ken's team had lost in the final seconds on a field goal. He was replaying the game in his head, wondering what made a certain play fail, and what play would have succeeded. As he pondered the difference between winning and losing that night, Josh sat quietly in the backseat, as focused as his father was on what had transpired that night.

"Dad, you know they were playing the radar defense," Josh piped up.

Ken paused. Of course, he knew that.

"Yes, Josh, I know they were playing radar," Ken said. There was a pause.

"Dad, on radar, the flats are open," Josh said.

"Yes, Josh, I know the flats are open on radar," Ken said.

There was another long pause, as if Josh was waiting for his father to say something. Finally, Josh leaned forward.

"Then, Dad, you probably also know you threw to the flats only twice tonight," Josh said.

Also as a seven-year-old, Josh would go with his father to Aberdeen Central High School at night.

"The lights would be off in the gym, but with the light from the clock you could just make out the rim on the basket," Josh said. "So I'd shoot for an hour or two while my dad worked in his office."

The Heupel's house on Apollo Avenue had a basketball hoop out front.

"We had a motion light that would go on, so that was good for playing at night," Josh said. "There were always people coming over to play basketball. I remember a couple of nights playing basketball in snowstorms."

And when he wasn't in football camps in the summer, he was in basketball camps.

When Josh was eight years old, his father took a job as an assistant coach at Northern State.

"Josh went with us everywhere," Ken said. "He was at practice, in meetings, films—everything. He was involved in every aspect of the program. He'd go with us the night before to stay in the hotel with the team. And from the first time Cindy decided it was okay for him to come to practice when he was two years old, and become involved, I never once had to say to him, 'Hey, cut it out.' He was always a part of the team, and the players seemed to really like him. He was like a coach, studying everything. The kid just loved the game. I remember telling Josh years later, 'Hey, I have to apologize for how busy I was while you were growing up, because I was climbing toward some coaching goals I had set, so I always took you to practice and everything when there was other stuff you probably wished we could have been doing.' Josh looked at me and said, 'Dad, my life has been the greatest it could be. I had the chance to do something I loved, football, with you. That's every kid's dream.' So the kid really let me off the hook."

Josh had a brief and successful wrestling career as well.

"He was the only undefeated wrestler in the country," Ken jokes. "He wrestled two tournaments when he was seven years old. I was an assistant wrestling coach at the high school level. He went to two kid's tournaments. He won the first one, going 3-0. At the second tournament, he won two matches to make the finals. We went outside in the school cafeteria to get a hot dog before the finals. He ate it, and said, 'I want to go home.' I said, 'Yes, and we will after this match.' He said, 'No, I'm done. We can go now.' He didn't like the way kids at that age grabbed around the throat. His passion wasn't there anymore. So that was it—he 'retired' right then and there."

In second grade, he told his mother that his mission in life was to help the poor and the homeless and troubled kids.

"Mom, I'm serious," Josh told her.

Cindy knew he was.

"He's known what his mission was for a long time," said Cindy, who is the principal at Aberdeen Central High School. "He was the first one to help a kid in class who needed it. He has an incredibly kind and compassionate heart. I was acutely aware of that—as an educator—because I would watch his psychology of learning and the various phases. He would always help the little one. When choosing teams for football, he wouldn't pick the best player; he would pick the one nobody wanted first so they would feel special. Our special education teacher told me that Josh would always reach out to the kids who were mainstreamed for P.E. or health class."

Ken's favorite recollection was a basketball tournament. Josh, age 10, brought his team back from a fourth-quarter deficit to win a tournament in Watertown, South Dakota.

"Josh hit a few crucial shots, and they won the thing," Ken said. "They started handing out the trophies."

The process slowed as the folks handing out the trophies realized they were one short. So they gave them to Josh and all of his teammates, except one little boy who didn't get to play much and sat on the bench most of the tournament.

"I was watching, wondering how they were going to handle being one trophy short," Ken said. "Josh went over to the kid who didn't get one and said, 'Here, you take mine—I can just get one next week.' That was Josh, always looking out for the underdog."

In fourth grade, Josh started playing in a flag football league. That's where his competitiveness and leadership continued to blossom.

"In the first flag football game he played, they were down by two touchdowns," Ken said. "He brought them back to win in the fourth quarter. You could see he had the touch to do it at the end. When a lot of players might shy away, Josh would step up at that critical time. Whether it was basketball, baseball, football or even hockey, he had that same competitiveness and leadership ability. He wanted the pressure on his shoulders. And he'd take it from there."

He also would enter tournaments in various other sports, including racquetball, a sport in which he won a tourney.

Since Aberdeen was in the northern part of the tornado range in the Midwest, the family always had to be prepared for that possibility. Grandma Gladys remembers those times of huddling in the basement and trying to make it fun so as not to scare the grandchildren.

"Actually, that basement was pretty cozy," Gladys said. "I'd make popcorn, and there was a mattress down there. The kids would play cards and games."

Josh has fond memories of growing up in the cozy, chilly confines of Aberdeen.

"I think Aberdeen is an awesome place to raise kids," Josh said. "It's a town of about 30,000, but it has everything you need or would want. The thing is, there is a sense of community. Your kids are safe. People leave their doors unlocked during the day. Anywhere you go, you know people. There's never been a time going out with Mom or Dad that we didn't run into someone we knew. Because of the tightness of the community, if there's someone in need, there's an outpouring of support."

While he was pushing himself on the field and on the court, Josh took the same work ethic into the classroom.

Josh took his schoolwork seriously.

"He devoured everything he did," Cindy said. "We wanted our kids to be balanced with faith, family, school and sports. But I never had to remind Josh to do his homework. He'd practice his reading words with his Dad, and then me. He'd read us stories."

The library was also a favorite stop for Josh. He participated in summer reading programs.

"He'd read every sports book he could get his hands on," Cindy said. "He liked biographies, too, like that of the Minnesota Vikings quarterback, Fran Tarkenton. He often read the same books over and over. He'd memorize what motivated these people to achieve, and note the paths they took to reach their goals."

3

A Near Tragedy Averted

On June 13, 1988, when Josh was 10 years old, the family had a very bad scare. Cindy woke with a bad headache at 5 a.m.

"I had never really had a headache, so I got up and took a couple of pills," Cindy said. "We know now that when the alarm clock went off at 6:00 a.m. to get Josh off to basketball camp, the blood clot was forming."

It was a blood clot on the right side of Cindy's brain.

"I got up out of bed to get Josh ready, and I walked into the wall because I was losing my motor skills and coordination," Cindy said.

Cindy was suffering a stroke. She was air-ambulanced to the University of Minnesota Medical Center where she had a six-hour surgery. She lost her coordination and had drop foot. She also lost use of her left hand and her peripheral vision. Cindy had to learn to walk and talk again.

She returned home nearly two weeks after the surgery. Andrea and Josh would go with her to therapy.

"I wanted my children to see that their mother would be fine and that nothing can stop you except yourself and your attitude," Cindy said. "I wanted them to know that we can all get through things if we smile and work hard."

Cindy couldn't do simple puzzles. It took her 90 minutes to find a name and number in the phone book.

"That's pretty scary for someone who did those things all the time," Cindy said. "Ken was incredible helping me with the physical therapy. My mother helped with some of the occupational things, such as reading and writing. I couldn't sequence numbers, so the kids and I would play games."

The first week that Cindy was home, Josh and Andrea slept on the floor of their parents' bedroom.

"We loved her and we were worried about her," Josh said. "We wanted to be there for her."

On Oct. 10, Cindy had a setback in her recovery when a seizure brought the police and paramedics to the house.

"That was very scary," Cindy said. "It was a direct result of the surgery."

But sisters Beth Bernard and Kathy Carr were there to help out. The two helped take care of Josh and Andrea through the years, with Kathy inheriting the job from Beth when Beth moved on and Kathy went to college at Northern State in Aberdeen.

"I couldn't drive, so the girls would pick up the kids and start dinner, those kinds of things," Cindy said. "We never got my anti-convulsive medication regulated, so I'd literally fall asleep in my food on occasion."

The experience made her family stronger. It also raised the awareness of their faith.

"We learned that if you raise your children to know God then they will have their faith to lean on later in life," Cindy said. "We found out how strong they were at handling adversity. Even at that age, Josh and Andrea had a very strong faith in God and knew that everything would be all right whether Mom lived or died."

It also brought out the importance of community, something that was abundant in Aberdeen.

"The community really rallied behind our family; someone was always helping my dad out, bringing over dinner, helping out the kids," Josh said. "I know living in a smaller town fosters that kind of thing. But I'd like to think that would happen no matter where you're at because there are good people who care about you."

Daughter Andrea said the illness brought even more perspective.

"It was a tough time in our lives," Andrea said. "Through that, it brought our family even closer. We learned not to take life for granted, to live each day to the fullest."

Some of Josh's fondest memories of the summers he had growing up were in Ashley at his grandparents' farm, that of Bertha and Theo Heupel—the same farm that had on its property the farmhouse Josh lived in the first six months of his life. Josh's father also had some land up there.

"He would go up with me, fixing fence," Ken said.

That was also where Josh learned the importance—one he translated to sports—of maintaining intensity and focus even when he grew tired later in the day.

"We were up there repairing and putting up some fence," Ken said. "And one day Josh said to me, 'You know, Dad, I've been watching you, and you kick it into another gear to finish the night out.' I think that's where he got the idea of putting extra time in when other people call it quits. Come on, anyone can put in eight hours a day. It's the guy who puts in that extra hour or two who gets ahead."

Josh says the work was backbreaking but it built character.

"That's where I learned what hard work really is," Josh said. "The first day is bad enough when you're fixing a fence, but getting up that second day is the true test because you're so sore. Of course, I had some of the best meals ever prepared by Grandma Bertha those days."

Grandma Bertha also remembers those times fondly. She

recalls running her stove all day, making food for her grand-kids.

"I'd make chocolate pudding, dough dishes, strudels, dumplings, chicken, sausage—everything the old German way," Grandma Bertha said. "Sometimes, when their parents came to get them, they would say, 'Wow, what happened to you guys?' They'd all put on weight from working hard and eating so well."

Ken agrees.

"I'll bet Josh put on 10 or 15 pounds each summer doing that," he said.

The granddaughters and grandsons would play inside their grandparents' house, which was barely recognizable when the grandkids took over.

"They have all the quilts and blankets out, building forts," Grandma Bertha said. "The boys took over the living room, and the girls had the dining room."

Ken says the work ethic will never be lost among the kids who put in time doing that work.

"By working that kind of atmosphere, you really establish a good work ethic," he said.

Grandma Bertha always made chocolate chip cookies for the kids before she'd visit Aberdeen. And when Josh visited, he'd spend time with his Grandpa Theophil before his grand-father passed away in 1997. The two often would go fishing together.

"Those were great times," Josh said. "I was very close to Grandpa. I learned a lot from him."

They'd head to Hoskins Lake near Ashley and catch all the Northern Pike they could. After the fish were cleaned, Grandma Bertha would put the fish in cornmeal and flour, and fry them up.

"Josh and his grandpa would go out and check the cattle, making sure all was well," Grandma Bertha said.

"We were blessed to be able to be in the grandkids' lives a lot," Grandma Bertha said.

Josh also was fond of Grandma Gladys' cooking.

"One time, I took 53 dumplings down to them, and Josh said, 'No one eat too much because I want them for leftovers,'" Gladys remembers. "Or at our house, he'd come in and tell his Grandpa Thomas, 'Grandpa, I want the biggest steak you've got.' Ken would say, 'Josh, you couldn't eat that.' And Grandpa would say, 'Sure, here you go, Josh.' And Josh would work his way through it as much as he could. Josh was always real close to both sets of grandparents."

Grandma Bertha also remembers going to Josh's games.

"After the game, Josh and his father would sit and talk about the game, going over everything from start to finish," Grandma Bertha said. "It was just unbelievable how much that boy and his father enjoyed doing that."

When Cindy's brother in law, Pat Parten, went to serve in the Gulf War as a captain in the U.S. Army, Julie Parten, who was pregnant, along with her and Pat's two sons, Jake and Zachary, moved in with Josh's family on Dec. 13, 1990.

"I don't know what I would have been like if someone moved in with me all of the sudden like that," said Jake, who was 10 when he moved in with Josh, who was 12 at the time. "I had to share Josh's room, and he really took me under his wing. He was an incredible shot in basketball. It seemed like he hardly ever missed. He taught me how to shoot a basketball."

Jake said one day that he and Josh even coerced a sick day out of Jake's mother, Julie Parten.

"My mom was pregnant, and we went to her saying we didn't feel that great," Jake says. "She let us stay home. We spent the day playing Nintendo, and my mom even got us hamburgers at Scotty's drive-in. We spent that whole day in our pajamas. It was one of the best days of my life. I know Josh never skipped a day of school before, or after, that one. But it was a great day."

And in February of 1991, Julie gave birth to her and Pat's daughter, Caitlin.

"Jake and Josh were like brothers," Julie said. "Zachary was just five years old. Josh really took good care of him. Whenever they played games, Josh would have Zachary on his team, and they'd play against Jake and Andrea."

Kathy Carr, and her sister, Beth Bernard, babysat and took care of Josh and Andrea through the years. Part of that meant taking Josh to his sporting events.

"Josh was so humble, and he was very serious about his sports," Kathy said. "On the days he had games, I'd be driving a group of the kids. And most of them would be messing around in the backseat, but not Josh—he was so focused. Even in junior high, he studied the other teams in town, and what they had done in their last games. While his friends goofed around, Josh went over strengths and weaknesses in his head for that day's game, thinking about what he'd do in certain situations."

Most of Josh's teams were quite successful.

"Josh's room had trophies galore from the time he was very little," Kathy said. "I think those meant a lot to him because they were team awards. He's had such a good head on his shoulders for so long."

4

'Working' at the Car Wash

Ken Heupel is a coach, inside and out. So he decided that when Josh got into junior high, the young man should learn what real responsibility was.

"My dad taught me to do things correctly, which was his way. I say that half jokingly," Josh said with a smile.

Josh admits he was slacking a little on the weekend. His father, unbeknown to Josh, called Lee Wilson, owner of the town's Deluxe Car Wash.

"I'm going to send Josh down for a job interview, if that's all right," Ken said on the phone. "Show him your toughest job."

Wilson agreed. So the next week, Ken talked to his son.

"It's time you got a job," Ken said.

Josh looked at his father, stunned.

"A job?" Josh asked. "Are you sure, Dad?"

Ken nodded.

"Call Mr. Wilson down at the car wash," Ken said. "See if you can get a job interview. Put on your best clothes, find a way to get down there and then interview with him."

Josh called Wilson, who scheduled an interview for that Saturday. On that morning, Josh got up, cleaned himself up and was dressed up nicely. He went down to the carwash to see Wilson.

During the bike ride down there, Josh realized it was unseasonably hot.

"It might have been one of the hottest days in the history of Aberdeen," Josh recalled. "It was over 100 degrees outside."

At the car wash, Josh filled out "a bunch of paperwork."

Then, Wilson took him into the soak room.

"If it wasn't 180 degrees in there, then it was 190," Josh remembers.

Young Josh wasn't ready for the working world.

"As I stood there in the soak room, I thought, 'There has to be a better way,'" Josh recalls. "That age—junior high—is a time when you think you can make your own decisions and do everything your own way. At that time, life really isn't that hard. Up until that point, I had always been given the opportunity to do what I wanted during the summer. I was getting kind of lazy."

He realized that standing in the soak room. Josh got home, still drenched from the humidity in the soak room. He saw his father in the yard as he got home.

"I get the point, Dad," Josh told him.

His father knew that many of Josh's friends were allowed to sleep in.

"That's why I did the car wash thing," Ken said. "I wanted Josh to know what was ahead of him if he didn't get the point. I told him, 'You're going to make a decision about what you're going to do, but you're not going to sleep until 10 or 11 each weekend morning like some of the other guys.'"

So on Saturday mornings, Josh was committed to his responsibilities.

"You know how on Saturday morning, you always want to sleep in?" Josh remembers. "At the break of dawn, my father would knock on my door. He didn't say who it was, but I knew. I heard this voice, 'Get up.' I'd sleep a little longer. But as soon as I heard that lawnmower crank up, I was running out the door."

Ken didn't think his son had grown overly lazy. However, he knew children that age didn't understand or appreciate responsibility.

"I deal with kids all the time as a coach," Ken said. "The ones who are successful have a great work ethic. If you can establish that in the kids at a young age, they're gong to be successful."

By high school, that work ethic had been more than honed. And that was a good thing because the program at Aberdeen Central had been on a slide when Josh started ninth grade.

Though his first school, Roncalli, a private Catholic school in Aberdeen, was a good school, playing in a public school meant a bigger challenge in terms of a higher competitive level. Josh went to Holgate Junior High for ninth grade, one of two public junior highs in Aberdeen. It was there he was told he was "too small" to play quarterback. He shook it off and was more ready than ever to prove himself the following year at Aberdeen Central.

"He has always worked hard and wanted to be at the next level," Cindy said.

He also liked the challenge of helping get Central back on the state's football map.

"We were a bad program, which was also part of the appeal," Josh said. "In recent history we were probably among the worst teams in the state consistently. There was a lot of appeal to be part of turning it around."

Succeeding at Central meant more because of the recent woes of the past.

"I think that's a mistake people make—trying to find the easy way to success," Josh said. "If you have the tools available, you can build or fix anything. We had the tools there. The turnaround at Aberdeen Central was something extremely memorable for me and everyone involved in the program and community at that time."

With Josh's leadership skills and knowledge of the game, quarterback was the logical position as it had been since his flag football day.

"He's always wanted the ball in his hands, making the decisions," Ken said.

Josh immediately became the starting quarterback at Aberdeen Central, though the team went just 3-6 his sophomore season.

"The program hadn't had a winning season in a decade," Head Coach Steve Svendsen said. "The program was really struggling when I took over the year before."

Things got worse, in part, during Josh's junior year. Though the team went 1-7, Svendsen saw improvement in some areas.

"We had Josh as our quarterback, and we decided to go young everywhere else and build something," Svendsen said. "Our offense scored a lot of points; it's just that we gave up a lot of points on the defensive side of the ball."

The parts were in place for more success during Josh's senior year.

"I changed defensive coordinators for that season, and we really got it turned around," Svendsen said. "We started an off-season program of throwing, and Josh was very involved in that. He was right alongside the coaches making calls to get kids out to throw and catch and work out. In fact, Josh's leadership was one of the best things about him. He knew what it took to be successful, and I don't think a lot of kids have that at that age. The goals he set were high, and that was part of his maturity."

That time was also the point where his cousin, Jake Parten, realized what everyone would be talking about down the road, about how Josh's commitment and preparation built him into such a good player that he brought up the level of the players around him.

"Josh thinks it is all right to get an accolade, but the biggest thing to him is, 'What have you done for the team and what is the team doing?' That's more important to Josh," Jake said. "Josh elevates everyone around him to be the best because he's such a competitor. He just makes everyone so much better."

Svendsen remembers some long nights at school with Josh.

"We would watch hour after hour of game film," Svendsen said. "I'd say, 'All right, Josh, I have a family at home, and I have to get out of here.' The kid was just so meticulous about game planning. He knew if he had an idea he could bring it to us. He knew defenses because of all the time that he had spent with his father when Ken was a defensive coordinator. Josh could just look at a play and tell you what was happening everywhere on the field. It was funny, we'd tell him a play once and say, 'OK, you've got it,' because we just knew he did. That's a coach's dream."

Josh is credited for "having a feel" for the game, a kind of "field sense" that helps him think and react quickly.

Some skills are taught, but others are more innate. Simply put, there are some things in sports that are learned, and some that, while honed through hard work, come naturally.

"We had a linebacker at Northern State who could blitz like no one else I've ever coached," Ken said. "I thought to myself, 'I can teach that.' It took me two years to find out that I couldn't. Every coach in America wants to and tries to teach those kinds of things that come with a feel for the game. But you either have it or you don't. Josh has that feel, that knack. He's done that his entire life since the first time he picked up a ball to hit a shot in basketball or to throw a pass."

Josh's senior year at Aberdeen Central High School was memorable. The team went 8-2 and lost to Brandon Valley in the state quarterfinals by one point. But the most painful loss came two weeks earlier in the conference championship at rival Yankton, a two-point loss.

"As far as I knew, Aberdeen had never beaten Yankton," Svendsen said. "Yankton was twice our size. Their offense was to grind the yards out on the ground. We ran the ball only four times the whole game. So we put the burden on the shoulders of Josh. He was just unbelievable, maybe the best high school game I've ever seen a kid play. It was back and forth all the way. Before the half, we were down by nine after Yankton scored with 32 seconds left in the second quarter. We got the ball on our 20 after they kicked off, and they thought we were just going to sit on it and let the half expire. But Josh made a good throw, so with nine seconds left we had the ball up to our own 40-yard line. Josh came over to me on the sideline. Together, we kind of drew up a play in the dirt. Josh made another heckuva throw, and we had a touchdown—the thing is, he throws a nice deep ball, which he never gets credit for. That kept us down by only two at the half. He took a lot of hits that game. He always stands in the pocket and has such great composure."

Aberdeen Central High School assistant principal Dean Kranhold remembers Josh's senior year fondly and also remembers that Yankton game.

"Josh's senior year was a terrific time for Central High School fans," Kranhold said. "CHS had not been a football power for many years but ran through the schedule with huge victories until they got to Yankton, South Dakota's football powerhouse. Yankton ran the ball and Aberdeen threw the ball. The game was at Yankton, and right before the game Aberdeen's top runner, pass catcher out of the backfield, and return man hurt his leg and was unable to play. The weather favored a ground game with high winds, rain, and sleet throughout the evening. Neither defense could stop the other team and Josh completed crucial pass after crucial pass to keep his Central team in the game. The lead seesawed back and forth and when time ran out, Yankton had victory.

"There are several things that have remained a constant since high school. One, preparation. He not only prepared himself, he prepared everyone on offense, especially in the summer time. No matter how hot, he was throwing to his receivers and working out every day. Two, the little swagger as he surveys the defense and steps up to the center. He had that as a sophomore. You just knew he was relaxed and the play would be successful and that the other team was scared as heck—they didn't know what was coming their way. High school defensive backs did not have a chance because Josh and the receivers communicated so well. Three, accuracy. Every kind of pass was on the money, even in the South Dakota winds. Four, humility. Credit was always given to everyone else, and they worked their butts off not to let him down. Five, temperament. I have never seen him display anything other than maturity and sportsmanship on the playing field. No ball slamming, kicking the turf, harsh words, etc. He was always as gracious in defeat as in victory. Josh set a standard for excellence in our community that has continued to influence our athletes. We finally made it to the state championship game in football for the first time in our history in 2000. Josh is a part of that."

Svendsen remembers Josh as a person as much as he remembers him as a football player.

"That quiet humility he has is so incredible," Svendsen said. "He's always been a competitor on the field."

While other kids looked up to him, they couldn't find him on the weekends.

"His classmates would go out to a party, and Josh would go to the weight room," Svendsen said. "His mother and father are two great people, and they've instilled those values and that work ethic. He has what they call those three F's—faith, family and football—and they're in that order. He does a nice job of keeping his priorities straight. Potentially, there are so many distractions. But that didn't faze Josh."

Svendsen will never forget Josh's commitment.

"He was driven to get to his goal," Svendsen said. "And his goal is to play on Sundays in the NFL. He'll get that done. This is a kid who was a skinny little sophomore, but had built himself up to 200 pounds as a high school senior through working out hard and eating right. He kept diaries of what he ate, and kept journals with all his workouts in them."

There is one part of Josh's tenure that Svendsen would just as soon forget, though.

"Before every game, the kid would throw up," Svendsen said. "It was part of the routine. Before the Yankton game, he hadn't yet, and I was getting nervous. The team was heading out to the field, and I was thinking, 'Come on, Josh, hurry it up.' Bless the kid's heart, he heaved right there. It made me feel better."

The community support was part of the reason the turnaround was so enjoyable.

"They really got excited about football again," Josh said. "It's amazing to see what success in an athletic endeavor can do to people on the team and in the community."

Relying on others was a prerequisite in high school football. That's a lesson Josh carries with him to this day.

"Any worthwhile journey takes a lot of hard work, and in a team sport it makes you realize the importance of trusting those around you," Josh said. "That's a big part of the lessons that I took with me from the experience at Aberdeen Central. I also learned to enjoy the hard work you put into building something. People get so caught up in the end accomplishment that they forget about the road that took them there. What you should enjoy the most is that path, that road—the journey itself. That's where the memories are made. You remember the places you've seen and people you've met. If you don't get the most you can out of the journey, then the destination—meeting your goals or not—feels pretty empty, especially after some time passes."

However, Josh nearly ended up playing basketball in college.

Julie thought Josh would be a college basketball player, especially after seeing him excel at Aberdeen Central, where he was on the varsity as a sophomore and a starter as a junior and senior.

"He was an awesome basketball player," Julie said. "I thought that's the way he'd go for a college scholarship. He was such a good three-point shooter. He brought that intensity to work as a team to get it done. Of course, that's the same thing he brought to the football team."

Dean Kranhold, Aberdeen Central's assistant principal, also thought Josh would have made a good college basketball player.

"He was an outstanding basketball player all through high school," Kranhold said. "He was the first one off the bench as a sophomore. He and Mike Miller, the Orlando Magic rookie (in 2000-01), used to do battle on the same court as high school opponents, although Mike is a little younger than Josh. I remember his coach saying that there wasn't another sophomore in the state that he'd rather have on his team than Josh. Josh could shoot, play defense, and make plays, showing the same leadership on the court as he did on the field."

With a lot of success as a high school basketball player, Josh would have had the opportunity to play college basketball.

"I was a pure shooter, and I really thought I was going to be a basketball player for a while," Josh said. "But I really enjoyed the game of football. I enjoyed the role of quarterback because it's the most unique position in sport. In football, you bring 100 people together from completely different backgrounds, with different size and speed—just different human beings. That made football more appealing to me than basketball."

5

Leaving The Nest

Late in his senior year of high school, Josh was faced with the biggest decision he'd had to that point: where to go to college and play football. Northern State wanted Josh. His father, an assistant coach at the time—he took over as head coach in 1997—said Northern State went after Josh.

"We recruited him hard," Ken said. "As his father, I stepped away and told our head coach that I would not recruit him. But the rest of the staff recruited him extremely hard. Josh made the decision to go to Weber State on his own."

The University of Montana and Weber State were the only Division I-AA colleges that were offering scholarships, though he did have a lot of contacts from Division II, Division III and NAIA schools.

"I wanted to challenge myself, and that meant playing at the highest possible level I could," Josh said. "That was probably the hardest decision I had to make. I learned a lot, though, about the process of making a big decision. You have to go through it analytically and then also follow your heart. My parents were very supportive, but they made it clear that it was my decision all the way because I was the one who has to live and follow through with it."

He picked Weber State because the passing school had a good tradition of throwing the ball, even producing several NFL quarterbacks.

"That was just the best place for me," Josh said. "They would have a senior quarterback heading into my first year, so I knew I could redshirt and really learn the system."

That system was the biggest part of the appeal, along with the coaching staff.

"That offense, places a lot of responsibility on the quarterback," Josh said.

So Josh went off to Weber State and learned the system, redshirting as planned. After the fall season, Josh entered spring football knowing he had a good chance to be the starting quarterback for that fall if he worked hard and demonstrated that he could run the offense.

But more competition was on the way. Steve Buck, a transfer from UCLA, had beaten out Cade McCown for the job there before breaking his hand, and then getting beat out the next year by McCown. Buck knew Weber State's history and transferred there in the spring of 1997.

"I was watching Arizona State and Ohio State in the Rose Bowl when I got the call that Buck was coming," Josh said. "So it was totally out of the blue. Steve had a real howitzer for an arm—just a missile launcher. I've never seen a guy with a stronger arm."

Weber State coach Dave Arslanian called with the news that Buck was on the way. Josh hung up the phone and went to his father, asking for the keys to the weight room at the college. He explained to his dad that Buck was on the way. Ken was well aware of who Buck was.

"So why do you want the keys?" Ken asked.

"I'm going to beat this guy out," Josh said.

Still, Josh pushed forward and was feeling good during spring ball.

But in a moment, his career was put on hold, almost taken away for good.

6

Overcoming Adversity

In Weber State's 1997 spring game, Josh tore the anterior cruciate ligament in his right knee.

"I wasn't hit or running hard or cutting or anything," Josh said.

Indeed, he wasn't even scrambling, just moving around in the pocket and the knee gave way.

The blown-out knee wasn't taken seriously at first by his family.

"I answered the phone when he called," Andrea said. "I said, 'How'd it go?' He said, 'I tore my ACL.' Josh is such a joker, so I said, 'Quit joking around; how'd you do?' It turns out he was serious. The way we look at it is, everything happens for a reason. God had a plan. Sometimes it's hard to recognize that. Look at where he is now. God brings obstacles in your life you have to overcome, whether it's football or other things."

The timing of the injury made it even more painful.

"That was hard because I felt so good with where I was, and how I was developing," Josh said. "I was competing hard for the job. The injury was just a freak accident. I didn't get hit or anything. The training staff took me to the locker room, and the doctor said, 'It's torn. Surgery.'"

It was like the air went out of Josh's lungs.

"The first 24 hours after the injury was the first time in my life where I was down and felt a little bit beaten up," Josh said. "I remember banging my hand against a wall, kind of asking, 'Why?' Then I called home. My dad asked, 'How did the spring game go?' I said, 'Well, Dad, not good, in fact …'"

Recovering from major knee surgery takes anywhere from nine months to a year—and sometimes longer. Josh had his own timeline. It was late April and two-a-day fall practices started in just over three months.

"Six months would have put me into October or early November before I came back," Josh said. "I knew I had to be back in time for two-a-days. That's all there was to it."

By the next morning, Josh and his father had a plan in place, one that could get Josh on a timeline to get back for the fall. Dr. Donald Shelborne in Indianapolis, Indiana, was a highly regarded surgeon.

The plan was to get the swelling down as much as possible before the surgery. However, Shelborne also knew that many patients needed a little longer to get into the right frame of mind, so he was planning on waiting at least a week, before the surgery.

Josh and his family wanted the surgery done as soon as possible because the few remaining months until fall practice were passing quickly. Every extra day spent waiting for surgery was setting Josh's rehab back an according number of days. Time was precious at that point.

"I'm going to visit with your son and do the surgery next week," Shelborne told Ken and Cindy. "In situations like this, the patient needs some time to get emotionally ready."

"You don't know Josh," Cindy told Shelborne. "He will be ready."

Shelborne was surprised the parents were so sure.

"Well, I'll meet with him tonight," Shelborne said, and that was Thursday.

Shelborne was impressed after talking with Josh.

"Well, your son is ready," Shelborne told Ken and Cindy that night. "He's a pretty amazing young man, focused and mature. We'll go ahead and push the surgery up to first thing Monday morning."

That Sunday was Mother's Day. Later that day, after the family saw a movie, a limping Josh announced his present for his mother.

"Mom," Josh said, "I'm going to take you on a carriage ride."

The horse-drawn carriage took them around downtown. Monday morning he was getting ready for surgery.

"Wait a minute, Mom," Josh said in the doctor's waiting room. "Take a picture of my knees."

His mother did.

"He just wanted to remember his knee without any scars," Cindy said.

Right after surgery, Josh was in good spirits.

"After you've been under anesthesia, your true personality comes out as it wears off," Cindy said. "Josh kept saying thank you to everyone. He was just incredibly kind. And, of course, the people there were just great."

Josh remembers those people fondly.

"I made a lot of great friends out there, some of the best people in the world are out there and we still stay in touch," Josh said.

Josh had successful surgery, but that was only part of the battle. The rest of the road was the long part, rehabilitation. Some of that was done twice daily at the rehab center in Indianapolis. But a good part of the range of motion activity was to be done by Josh and his father several times a day in their hotel room.

Ice packs were applied every 20 minutes.

"Every hour had a routine," Cindy said. "It was very intense."

The first 24 hours went smoothly.

"The first day was good, but on the second day, I could barely move the knee," Josh said. "The plan at that point was for my mom to stay the first week and my dad would then stay until my rehab was complete."

However, as Ken worked on his son's knee, Cindy could only watch helplessly as Josh bit down on a towel in pain, tears running down his cheeks.

"Needless to say, she shed a couple of tears," Josh said. "Dad and I looked at each other, and we both knew what the other was thinking."

Cindy remembers the image vividly.

"It was pretty awful," Cindy said. "I had tears in my eyes. Here is my child, biting on a towel, and more weight is being pushed on his knees. Ken was pushing Josh because both of them knew how important it was. Ken knew what Josh wanted and needed. In that regard, his dad really came through for him. But watching that …"

So Ken reluctantly expressed his and Josh's feelings.

"We need to get you on a plane home," he said to his wife.

"She was on the next plane back to South Dakota," Josh said. "It would have just been too tough on her to see me going through that several times a day. It was physically so very painful, but it was necessary. We all knew it. But it would have been too much to put my mom through to watch it time after time."

After Cindy left, Josh and his father were alone in the hotel room. They were grating on each other every day, more and more as time went on.

"Thank God, we had rehab twice a day down at the center," Josh said, "because we would have never made it through otherwise. We were really wearing on each other. We'd have choked each other if we didn't have the rehab. Those two weeks in Indy after my mother left were the two longest weeks of my life."

It was almost made short, by accident—literally.

As the two headed to one of the twice-daily rehab events a week after the surgery, the two were disagreeing about, of all things, the speed with which Ken was pushing Josh's wheelchair.

"My father," Josh said, "was driving me nuts."

So Josh offered his thoughts.

"You're going too slow," Josh said. "We've got more than a block left. Go faster."

The curbs in Indianapolis are sloped toward the street to direct runoff to the drain. As Josh's father heard his son's comments, he had a thought of his own.

"Fine," Ken said, "wheel yourself."

Ken gave Josh a firm push to get him started. However, Josh sailed right into the multi-lane one-way street.

"It was like a game of 'Frogger,' where you have to steer in and out of one-way traffic across a busy street," Josh said. "Cars were just buzzing all around me."

If the story sounds like tough love, it's because … it was.

"If you put it any differently or try to soften it, people who know Ken will know you're not telling the whole story," Cindy said. "That's just what happened. Those are two very strong-willed men. And it came out that day."

Shelborne just shook his head in amazement at Josh's progress, which was aided by his father's intense commitment to the rehabilitation.

"Dr. Shelborne said Josh had the fastest recovery of anyone he'd ever done the surgery on," Cindy said. "Josh gave credit to Dr. Shelborne and God."

When Josh got home to Aberdeen to continue rehab, he again surprised his father.

"He knew he had only about eight weeks to get ready," Ken said. "So 12 days after the surgery, we went home to South Dakota. The first day we were home, he hopped over an 8-foot fence at our practice field at Northern State. The only reason I knew is because he had cut his hand hopping the fence. I went in, and Andrea came out of the bathroom, where there was some blood. I said, 'What happened?' As much as she didn't want to, Andrea let the cat out of the bag. 'Josh cut his hand,' she said."

Ken finally tracked down Josh.

"What are you doing?" Ken asked. "You just had your ACL tear, and you're jumping fences?"

Josh looked at his hand, and then at his father.

"Dad," Josh said, "it's your fault."

"What?" Ken asked, astonished, "how's it my fault?"

"Well, it was locked," Josh answered. "The gates weren't opened, and I had to throw."

Josh had dumbbells in his bedroom that he worked out with each night, working on his upper body strength. He also did hundreds of pushups.

He continued his rehab, pushing himself so hard that his father winced just watching him.

"He was doing bags and cutting drills just four days after we got home," Ken said. "I was so scared. I said, 'Josh, are you really supposed to be doing this stuff?' He'd just keep going. The kid had a vision. He was just so focused."

Amazingly, Josh was back at Weber State as he had promised in August. There was no swelling at all in the knee, though it did get sore, and Josh iced it. He took a little more than a week off to let the healing process catch up. And by midseason in 1997, he was the quarterback for Weber State.

"I started playing well at the end of the year," Josh said. The season ended, and Josh was just getting started.

"I was really looking forward to coming back and competing the next year for the starting job," Josh said. "But ..."

Weber State's head coach accepted the same position at Utah State, and his staff went with him to Utah State. An entire new coaching staff was brought in.

"I knew a little about the staff before I got to meet with them," Josh said. "Then I met with them, and watched film to get prepared. However, I could tell that the offense wasn't geared toward the quarterback being really involved in the game. With that in mind, I knew it wasn't the best system for me. I knew that to continue my growth as a quarterback, I'd have to leave. I knew I should transfer as soon as possible so I could learn a new system and establish myself a little."

Ken said he knew it was hard for Josh to leave Weber State, but he has no doubt it was the right move.

"He loved the place and loved the coach," Ken said. "When they brought in the new coaching staff, they brought in a whole new offense. That is the only reason he left. He made some great friends there, though."

Josh could have transferred to a number of Division I-AA or Division II or III schools and played right away. However, that wasn't his plan. He wanted to play in Division I-A.

"I still wanted to compete at the highest level possible," Josh said. "But I knew if I went to a Division I school right away, I'd have to do what the NCAA rules state, and that meant sitting out for a full year. I had just come off a decent season after the knee surgery, and the year before that I had redshirted. So I wanted to play. That's why I went from a private school in eighth grade to a public school, Aberdeen Central, as a high school freshman—because I wanted to compete at the highest level. I've always wanted to measure myself against the best. I never wanted to say, 'You know, I bet I could have ...' or anything like that. I didn't want to have any doubts in my mind."

That meant going to a junior college in the spring of 1998. Josh looked around, and heard that Snow College in tiny Ephraim, Utah, though remote in location, had a good reputation as being a competitive, pass-oriented program. In fact, Josh's father, Ken, the football coach at Northern State (South Dakota) College had a few players from Snow.

So for Josh, everything pointed to Snow—and lots of snow, as it turned out.

7

Warm Hearts In Snow

Snow (Junior) College and its host town of Ephraim, Utah, are off the beaten path.

Way off it, in fact.

"It's surrounded by hills and mountains," Josh said. "It's right out of a movie, just desolate and cold. It was also one of the best years of my life."

However, it was also a great period of adjustment.

"I went from being on scholarship to not being on one," Josh said. "So I was giving up certain things for the uncertainty of no scholarship at that point, and perhaps not one even in the future."

Living in a Rocky Mountain outback meant sparse living. The dorm rooms were tiny, and the beds of similar scale. Many of the students were from nearby areas and escaped home on the weekends.

"But considering how far I was from Aberdeen," Josh says, "I wasn't going home. It was an eye opener. At first, I didn't know if I could do it."

Char Akkerman, a close friend of the family who is an assistant principal at Aberdeen Central, was able to visit Snow with Cindy and watch Josh play.

"I've never known a human being, at any age, who was so goal-oriented. He's been through some adversity," Char said.

"He never gave up on his dream. I got the privilege of going to Utah and watching him play at Snow. My goodness, what that kid went through to follow his dream. We had bigger crowds at Aberdeen Central than they did that day at Snow. The facilities were … well, it just broke my heart, not that they were bad people, or it was a bad place or anything. Josh is all about making friends, and he made some lasting friends at Snow."

Joe Borich was the quarterback coach at the time Josh went to Snow before Borich moved on to Idaho State.

"Snow is one of those special places where anybody who gets there says, 'Look at this place!' when they first arrive," Borich said. "They think the place will be awful because there's nothing to do. Yet whenever someone leaves and you hear from them again, they're always talking about how much they miss it. There's not a lot to do. So what you do is, you meet some great people and you can find yourself."

He did have football, and that was looking promising at first.

"I made sure before I went there that I'd have an opportunity to at least compete for the job right away," Josh said. "I knew if there was a starter coming back, it would put me behind the eight-ball, and I didn't have time for that. I had only one year to play there since I had been at Weber State and played one season."

The quarterback who had preceded Josh at Snow was Fred Salanoa, who had a lot of success the previous year, earning a full-ride scholarship to Hawaii.

"With Fred being gone, there was no doubt there would be an opening for a quarterback," Josh said. "They had a great system and great coaches, and the program had been very successful."

Borich said he's never seen a quarterback like Josh.

"To me, he's the perfect quarterback," Borich said. "He's the best quarterback I've ever seen from the shoulders up. He understands the game so well. He knows the little things it takes to succeed. Josh understands that he has to learn the offense, be a leader and stay composed—and that is Josh in a nutshell. He knows he doesn't have to complete every pass for 90 yards. He sees what the defense is doing and what we can take from that, and then puts the ball into our athletes' hands. Josh really grasps that."

Josh's leadership ability was nurtured at Snow.

"A lot of 18- or 19-year-olds want to play quarterback because they get all the glory," Borich said. "Not Josh. He's doing it because he wants to lead. He earns respect. His teammates just love Josh. He has a quality about him that tells his teammates that they are more important than anything else and he will sacrifice for them. We had kids from the Island of Samoa, Los Angeles, Miami and Tacoma, yet all of those kids followed Josh as their leader. There was such an admiration for him. There's no doubt this was Josh's team the year he was at Snow."

Josh won the starting quarterback job with a solid performance during spring football. He was getting ready to head home for the summer when the coaches called him in.

"It was just two days before summer vacation," Josh said.

Fred had found out things weren't going to be how he thought at Hawaii, so he called back to Utah to find out if he could return for another season.

"So what it meant was he was coming back to Snow for a second year," Josh said. "I was going to be forced to compete for the job against a guy who had been an All-American at Snow the year before and had thrown for 3,000 yards and 30 touchdowns."

Josh looked at the coaches and asked what this meant.

"You will have to compete for the starting job," the coaches told him. "But we're not putting Fred in as the starter right now. You will still have the opportunity to be the starter."

The coaches were ready to welcome Fred back, but they also knew they had found their man in Josh.

"That was really potentially a very difficult situation," Borcih said. "Fred had led the nation in offense the year before. So when things didn't work out at the University of Hawaii, he called us at Snow and said he wanted to come back.

"We told Fred, 'Hey, we've got a guy. You'll have to come in and beat Josh out.' Josh has earned the starting job."

When Salanoa arrived, the coaches were amazed at what transpired.

"Fred and I became the best of friends," Josh said. "He's a great competitor, a great athlete and a caring person."

Borich and the coaching staff were more than pleased.

"It was unbelievable how well it worked out," Borich said. "Josh started every game. He played so well in the first half that by the second half, when Fred was put in, we were usually quite comfortably ahead. So we had a first-team All-American as our backup quarterback. But that those two handled it so well really said something about them. It tells you how much football and team meant to them."

The film-study sessions were frequent. And Borich never had to track Josh down at the set time.

"I just remember little things more than anything else," Borich said. "We'd decide to meet at 10 a.m. He was always there by 9:30. So one day, I show up earlier, and what do you know? He's already there with a smile, saying, 'Hey, coach, come on, we've got work to do. Where have you been?' Of course, he wore the same pair of sweats the whole time he was there, and I never saw him comb his hair once. But he accomplished everything he set out to."

The season was memorable for a lot of reasons. One was off the field where there were none of the luxuries that most Division I-A—and I-AA, for that matter—colleges have.

"The thing I remember about Snow, besides the football season, were the bus trips," Josh said. "We'd leave for 17-hour bus trips on Thursday nights to get to games. We'd sleep on the bus."

In the fall, Josh moved out of the dorm.

"I had seven roommates, and my room was about the size of a king-sized bed, so it was really cramped quarters," Josh said. "We were from completely different backgrounds. Four of the guys were returning from missions, so they were older, maybe 22 or 23 years old. We had a couple of younger guys. That house—and our whole football team at Snow—was a melting pot of people. That was the most enjoyable thing about it. I learned about people who were different from me. So I was able to learn to celebrate diversity and learn from people who had backgrounds that differed from mine."

That being said, Josh still recalls Snow with nothing but a smile.

"Now, after hearing everything else, everyone is thinking that I can't look back on the experience at Snow very happily," Josh said. "They think I was happy just to get out of there. But looking back at it, it was one of the most meaningful experiences of my life. It always gives me a huge smile whenever I'm talking with someone about Snow. I genuinely enjoyed the simplicity of life and football there. We didn't have thousands of fans at our games. We weren't getting a ton of media exposure. We had a lot of great players, and we were just going out playing football."

The team went 8-2 and blew out rival Dixie (Utah) in a junior college bowl game, 40-20.

"It really was a good season," Josh said. "We came up

short in a crucial game at the end of the year. But aside from that, it couldn't have been any better."

Something else happened at Snow that fall as well.

"I woke up one day and wasn't liking what I saw in the mirror," Josh said. "It was there at Snow that I completely gave God control of my life. That helped my situation because I really ended up enjoying it there."

First the knee surgery, and then the trip to barren Snow. It gave Josh a second lease on his football life. More importantly, it gave him perspective.

"Part of my upbringing was realizing that things can be taken away from you at any moment," Josh said. "So I really realized that I had to learn to enjoy the road and not just the destination because so much goes into it."

The time at Snow gave him renewed spirituality. And though it was only a year, the circle had closed.

"There comes a point when things are complete," Josh said. "After one year, my time in junior college was complete. It was time to move on."

A couple of his teammates from the 1998 team ended up at Northern State playing for Ken Heupel.

"We were all excited about the different directions we were headed," Josh said.

Josh was ready to play Division I-A football. He narrowed his list quickly to three: New Mexico, Utah State and Oklahoma.

"There were specific things I was looking for at a university," Josh said. "I wanted a major university that met my academic needs, that also would be a good fit for me athletically. Because of that, there were only a few schools that would be a fit."

Utah State was a perfect fit.

"The coaching staff at Weber State was at Utah State by

then, so I knew the offense in detail," Josh said. "Yet I knew from the moment I stepped on campus, that while it was a good fit, it wasn't a perfect fit."

New Mexico had a few other intangibles.

"New Mexico is a great state and it had great weather, which was appealing after living in Aberdeen and then at Snow in Utah. They had a good coaching staff. And a good offensive system, which placed pressure on the quarterback, and that was what I was looking for. But I found I was looking for something else."

Something farther east. And something bigger, as in the Big 12 Conference.

8

A Sooner at Last

And then, Josh Heupel visited Oklahoma. He loved the climate, immediately found the people of Oklahoma to be among the nicest he ever encountered, and he liked the Sooners' new coaching staff.

Josh met with Oklahoma's recently hired head coach Bob Stoops, who had a lot of success at Kansas State and Florida as a defensive coordinator before taking over at Oklahoma.

"I spent 90 minutes with Coach Stoops when I had my campus visit," Josh said. "I asked him if he thought they could win the Big 12 Conference championship and compete for the national championship. He said yes, and by the look in his eyes, I knew he was certain. As soon as anyone talks with Coach Stoops, they can get an understanding of the commitment to success at Oklahoma."

Aside from that 90 minutes, Josh was with offensive coordinator Mike Leach the rest of the recruiting trip. Leach, who had been at Valdosta State, a small Division II college just two years earlier, went to Kentucky with head coach Hal Mumme. It was there Leach helped shape Tim Couch into one of the country's top passers, in addition to eventually being the top player taken in the NFL draft by the Cleveland Browns.

"I spent 98 percent of my time with Coach Leach," Josh

said. "We talked for hours on end, watching film of Tim Couch. I got a feel for what they wanted in a quarterback and for what their offense was going to allow a quarterback to do. And Coach Leach had the ability to see what I was going to bring to the table."

Leach remembers spending seven hours with Josh in their first meeting watching film on the recruiting trip.

"I knew there was something special about him when he came on his recruiting visit," said Leach, who moved on after one year at Oklahoma to become the head coach at Texas Tech. "We squeezed in a dinner or two. Mostly, we watched film. I offered to take him out and see some other stuff, and he said, 'Coach, I'd rather sit in here and watch film.' We spent six hours that first day watching film. So I thought he'd back off the next day. He came in and said, 'Can we go through some more film?' He wanted to learn the whole time. We ended up squeezing in a couple more meals watching film."

No other position offers the kind of responsibility that quarterback does.

"I firmly believe that a quarterback, in the right type of system, has the ability to lose a game on his own," Josh said. "To win, you need 10 others. Because of that responsibility, it is necessary—even vital—that I prepare myself the best I can each and every week. That's why I prepared myself with every ounce of energy. I was once told a story of a coach who had a backup quarterback who didn't prepare himself one week. The starter went down on the first play, and the back-up had to go in. This college football team needed to win this game to get into the playoffs. The backup quarterback went out there and played extremely poorly, to say the least. He was not able to move his football team at all. They lost the game. To this day, the guy still feels bad. When he had to look his teammates in the eye after the game, he looked at them with a sense of shame because he not only did a disservice to himself, but even more importantly, to the 90 other people who were counting on him. In life, it is too easy to give up on yourself, and accept failure. But it is hard to do that for 90 other people."

While a lot has been written about how Josh is student of the game because of his father's coaching career, Ken Heupel isn't so sure.

"I don't know if people really have an affect on something like that," Ken said. "Either a young man has it or he doesn't. It's more than just sitting in front of a video and watching it. A lot of people have put in that kind of time, but not many study it like he does."

Though Oklahoma wanted Josh, not a lot of other big-time colleges were pursuing him.

"He wasn't on as many lists as a lot of the other quarterbacks were," Leach said. "But we knew we needed a self-starter, a guy who could take a lot of it on his own shoulders. Because especially in the off-season when coaches can't contact the players, you need a guy among the players who can spearhead that because they need to be out every day running and throwing. That person was Josh. That first spring, he was at OU two months, and his teammates elected him captain."

Leach said coaches long for players like Josh.

"Josh is just an incredible student of the game," Leach said. "He studies the game constantly. The thing he has is the ability to analyze plays and go beyond the initial read. He knows which defender will go where in a certain situation. That got him out of a lot of bad situations because he knew where most everyone would be. He never gets rattled, and he's just a tireless worker."

Leach also appreciated Josh's rural roots, from growing up in South Dakota to his time at Snow College.

"I always ask him how things are going in Mystery, Alaska, because after seeing that show, I figured Aberdeen was kind of like that," Leach said with a smile.

For Josh's senior season at Oklahoma, he had another new coach, Chuck Long, a former University of Iowa star who played in the NFL for the Detroit Lions.

"I really enjoyed not only coaching him but getting to know him and his family," Long said. "Although I was with him for only one year, I feel like I've known him my whole life. I try to get to know the players beyond football. With Josh, that was easy. To his credit, he's had to go through two different coaches in two years at Oklahoma. So he could have had the attitude, 'I know the system, and I don't need to learn anymore.' But he wasn't that way at all. He wanted to learn more and get better as a football player."

That eagerness to learn is something that will continue to serve Josh well.

"The words 'settle for' are not in Josh's vocabulary," Long said. "There are some quarterbacks out there with egos who think they know it all. With his upbringing, he has no ego. He knows what he wants each and every day. It was my job to get the most out of him every day."

The big-game experience he had at Oklahoma, and even at Snow, also will serve Josh well.

"Josh's toughness was really something this year—he never complained," Long said. "The other thing he's done well is produce under pressure. He always produced when the pressure was on. There was pressure against Kansas State and then against Nebraska. After that it only intensified because everyone was gunning for us. It's not just the statistics he put up. It was the intangibles that were so impressive. He was a great leader for us. The guys not only rallied behind him, they took care of him, too, as everyone saw when our defense really stepped it up."

Long said that point was never more apparent than the Oklahoma State game, the last regular-season game.

"Our offense struggled, and Josh's head was down in the locker room because he likes to take the pressure on his own shoulders," Long said. "One of our great linebackers, Torrance Marshall, went up to him in the locker room at that game and said, 'Hey, Josh, get your head up. You've taken care of us for a long time, let us on the defense take care of you now.' That really showed me what kind of a leader Josh is. When you work the hardest, people will follow suit."

And like Josh's coaches from the past, Long will never forget the film-study sessions with Josh.

"I'd see him late at night in the film room," Long said. "And I remember in the spring of 2000—it was a Friday in March—when most of the players would lift in the morning and then be done, having the weekend off. Josh got a few of his receivers, calling them up on the phone—because the coaches aren't allowed contact with the players at that time. Josh would call them up and say, 'Let's go out and throw.' Josh was in charge of all that. I remember looking out the window and seeing Josh on that cold, windy afternoon. That really told me a lot about Josh Heupel."

Long knows what it takes to be an NFL quarterback.

"Josh shapes up very well," Long said. "He has a great mental capacity. He can absorb a lot more football knowledge than most quarterbacks. So he'll be well ahead of the game in that regard when he's in the NFL. His NFL coach will realize this young man is years ahead of his time. His mental capacity alone will allow him to have a long career."

While Josh is blessed with plenty of physical talent, it is the other factors that will enable him to fit in at the NFL level.

"Everyone wants the kind of arm John Elway has, but

those guys are few and far between," Long said. "What gets you the championship are the quarterbacks with the mental capacity who know where to go with the football. He'll be playing in an era that's far different from the NFL that I played in because there are so many blitzes, and that's where he excels. Josh knows how to read defenses, and he's great off the scramble. He'll benefit from some great teaching in the NFL. Once that mixes with his knowledge and ability to pick things up, he'll flourish."

He has never been wary of taking the necessary steps to reach the next level.

"Josh has always had a goal to go to the next level," said his high school coach, Steve Svendsen. "He does everything possible, gets better, and moves on to the next challenge. He sets a goal, gets a plan, and sees it through. He believes in himself and just goes after it. That got him to high school to start as a sophomore, to start as a redshirt freshman at Weber, to be a star at Snow College, and then to be a Heisman Trophy finalist at Oklahoma. That's why he'll do well in the NFL. He's prepared and ready for that challenge, and he'll keep doing everything he can to get better."

His offensive coordinator the first year at Oklahoma, Mike Leach, agrees.

"I look at the arm issue this way," Leach said. "If you can throw the ball 60 yards on a line, that's great. If that's the requirement, then Joe Montana would have been out of the business the first year. Why do you have to throw it 60 yards? Because I've never coached a receiver who can run 60 yards in three seconds—and three seconds is about how long a quarterback has to throw it on most plays. The only time really a ball is thrown 60 yards is when it's a broken play. There are three reasons, actually: First of all, the quarterback might throw it 60 yards if the quarterback doesn't make a decision and gets a bunch of extra time to throw it. The second reason is if the receivers don't make a break and get open like they're supposed to. The third reason would be if the guard gets beat, and the quarterback is forced out of the pocket because by that time, everyone has time to get way down field. But it doesn't always happen like that. In most offenses, the quarterback goes through his reads very quickly and has to get the ball to a particular point at a particular time. And Josh excels at that."

9

A Loving Sister and Family

Football is a big part of Josh's life. But his faith and family top the list.

His little sister is his biggest fan, and vice versa.

"I admire Andrea so much," Josh said. "Andrea is someone I really look up to. She is very confident, a person of great substance. As young as she is, she already has a really strong idea of self—of who she is, and who she wants to be."

Andrea said the two complement each other.

"He always was, and still is, my best friend," Andrea said. "He always makes me smile. He always makes me look at life in a different way. Our parents brought us up as two different individuals. They treat us equal, yet they know we have two different lives."

Josh majored in business administration while Andrea is at the University of Oklahoma studying pre-med/micro-biology. Andrea knows her brother better than anyone else. She's seen him dance to N'Sync videos and just about anything else one could imagine.

"He can dance," Andrea said with a smile, "but I don't know about the singing part. He thinks he can sing, and he's my brother—I love him. But I'm not sure he can sing."

Andrea was also there when Chris Weinke of Florida State—which Josh and Oklahoma would defeat a month later in the Orange Bowl for the national championship—won the Heisman Trophy in New York. Josh finished second.

After the ceremony, the family had dinner in New York.

"You know Andrea," Josh told her, "if I'd have won this, my life could have taken a whole new twist. I would have always been known as a Heisman Trophy winner."

"But that's not who you are," Andrea said as Josh nodded in agreement.

The family agreed the Heisman wasn't destined for Josh.

"That's not who Josh is, and winning the Heisman wasn't his goal," Andrea said. "Football is not his life. It's just a part of his life."

Besides, Josh and Oklahoma won the "team Heisman"— the national championship trophy.

The two kids weren't insubordinate.

"They had a great respect for their parents," Cindy said. "I never felt like they took advantage of us or have taken us for granted. They always cherished their parents and respected our opinion. They have a mutual admiration for each other. Andrea will tell you Josh is her role model, and Josh will tell you likewise about Andrea."

Josh and Andrea still consider each other a best friend.

"They have such respect for each other, and they always did," Cindy said. "There was no competitiveness—no putting each other down to make themselves look good. We didn't tolerate that."

That's no surprise to former babysitter Kathy Carr.

"Josh and Andrea have been best friends since I've known them," Kathy said. "They are so devoted to each other. Josh doted over Andrea when she was little. And Josh just loved the way Andrea doted over him when she got older."

There have been a lot of times where perspective helped heal any real or perceived wounds. Part of that perspective comes from the small-town lifestyle that helped shape Josh's and Andrea's values.

The rural upbringing was a good nurturing environment.

"Certainly, there are pros and cons to the small-town life," Cindy said. "Your faith and family lay the groundwork, so no matter where you are raised, that comes into it. It's important to have active parenting and grandparenting, as well as that kind of interaction with aunts and uncles and cousins. In the small-town atmosphere, there are a lot of advantages. For example, I didn't have to worry about my children's safety. I knew where Andrea and Josh were, and whom they were with. Of course, there's that age where the independence starts to develop, too. But Josh and Andrea were trustworthy, so we allowed them some freedom and independence. You can't have your kids under your thumb the whole time. I admire and learn from my children—and I always have."

While Josh and Andrea receive a lot of accolades, their parents are prouder of them for the kind of people they have become.

"The thing we've always been proudest of is the way they treat people," Ken said. "Josh and Andrea are good, nice people. I remember after the Texas Tech game (in 2000), Josh brought me down toward the locker room. Everyone is patting him on the back for the game. And what does Josh do? Well, there was a food drive going on. So he goes over to the guy who is collecting food and says, 'How much food did we get?' Those are the things that Cindy and I get most excited about. I can't tell you how many times we've seen an elderly person or someone who is struggling, and then we'll see our son or daughter put in a nice word or gesture. That means the most. Football? That will come and go. You are on the field for a short period of your life. But, hopefully, you're a good person."

Char Akkerman is the assistant principal at Aberdeen Central.

"I've had reporters ask me, 'Come on, he had to do something wrong in high school; what was it?'" Char said. "Well, he didn't—not that I know of. He's a sweetheart. People think he can't be real, but he really is. And what is impressive is he's been that way from a young age. What's fun is to see someone who is so good stay so true to his dream, and do it in the right way. There's not a selfish bone in his body. Yes, he's driven to his dream. But he's not selfish—this is just what he wants in life."

And that was nurtured by a very special bond with his father.

"More than anything, I remember going to Josh's games," said Josh's uncle Wil, who is Ken's brother. "When he was playing high school basketball, they went to the state tournament his junior year. They lost in the first round to a team they were ahead of and supposed to beat. Josh was being his quiet, reflective self afterward. The thing you learn over time is to give Josh space and room before games and after games. He's always been able to shake it off pretty well. Another thing you learn is not to get in the way of post-game conversation between him and his dad. They have a really special relationship, a unique way of dealing with the things that went right and wrong in the game. Ken expects a lot of Josh, and Josh expects a lot of Josh. So I learned not to get in the way of that relationship."

Another reminder came after another home game in Norman in the fall of 2000.

"Were sitting there at a restaurant, and wanted to get going," Ken said. "I watched him sign all of these autographs, and spend a lot of time with young people. This woman came over, and had this boy with her. She said, 'Hi, Josh, you probably don't remember, but this is my son and you visited him while he was getting cancer treatment.' Josh remembered and started talking about it. The mother couldn't believe it. This young man was a third- or fourth-grader, and his face just lit up. They went back to sit down, and the young man came back again and thanked Josh for remembering him and visiting him."

The important thing to Cindy and Ken is that their kids really do know that everyone is created equal, and should be treated as such.

"What I'm proud of, is that Josh and Andrea don't see old or young, white or black, rich or poor," Ken said. "They know everyone is the same."

10

At Home In Oklahoma

There are much easier paths than the route I have taken—playing Division I-A college football. You can apply that to life. Any challenge will take a lot of effort and passion. You have to love what you are doing.

At Oklahoma, I would wake up, go for a morning run, go to classes and then lift weights or have practice. Then I would go to the film room. After that, I had to study for school. The demands on your body and mind are so great that if you don't love it, there's no way to force yourself through it. You will sell yourself short. You will sell your coaches and teammates short. You will sell the school short.

I never could have foreseen the kind of home that Norman, Oklahoma, would become to me. The people of Oklahoma have embraced me and made this my home. I always see myself coming back to Oklahoma. I don't know how or when. But I do know that I will be back because Oklahoma has been a huge part of my life.

Just a couple of months after arriving at Oklahoma in the spring of 1999, I was elected a team captain. That's the highest honor that I've ever received in team sports. To be a leader you have to be both a vocal and non-vocal leader. You have to be the hardest worker. You have to be the first one in and the last one to leave.

You have to be selfless instead of selfish. You have to genuinely care about the people around, and your teammates have to see that and feel that. Every ounce of energy you have has to go to ensure success for yourself and your teammates. When they know you've done everything humanly possible to make them successful, they will have complete confidence in you, which will allow them to play at the highest level.

Confidence comes from hard work. Knowing that you've paid the price to be successful, that you've done everything possible to make sure things go the way you envisioned them, is important.

We made a bowl and went 7-5 in 1999. But other than the Colorado loss, we should have won all of our games. That's part of what drove us to prepare for the 2000 season. We were anything but satisfied with our first season. Yes, we got ourselves into a bowl game. But we truly believed we should have, or could have, been playing for much more than we were playing for at the end of the year.

The long-term goal was still in place, so we kept taking one step at a time. Once we set our long-term goals, we looked to only the near future. We could take only one thing at a time. We respected everything in the process.

Still, losing was hard. I never take a defeat very well. I wasn't the friendliest person on Sunday after we lost. That losing was part of the process, though. And the team grew from those defeats.

That first season was a learning experience. There's a certain learning curve—learning to win—that has to run its course when a program hasn't won in a while. We didn't know how to finish off our opponents that season. The season ended with a last-second loss to Mississippi in the Independence Bowl, 27-25. Ending the season with a loss on a last-second field goal was extremely difficult.

To come as far as we did in two years was a great accomplishment, one that Coach Bob Stoops directed.

When I came on campus, everyone in the football program was headed in his own direction. Coach Stoops and his staff got everyone to buy into one vision and be on the same page and work toward that vision. I firmly believe that our success came about because no one worked harder than we did as a football team, including our off-season and preseason conditioning programs, as well as our preparation every week.

11

Faith Conquers All

As I mentioned earlier, my Christian walk started to mature at Snow. I just knew there was more to life—more peace and more joy about what was going to happen each day. When you wake up and it's not easy to get out of bed, or you're not excited about what could happen each day, you need to make a change. I had tried everything my own way to try to make it easy to get out of bed. But none of that had worked. Nothing had filled that void I was seeking to fill. It was almost as a last resort that I completely turned myself over to God.

Here are a few of my favorite readings, and what they mean to me:

Isaiah 54:17 *No weapon formed against you will prevail...*

This really became something that stuck in my head when I first got to the campus here at the University of Oklahoma. Not because of the players or coaches, but I realized how many people were doubting me as a football player or as an individual. There is lots of skepticism at the Division I-A level, where the media and microscope are more intense. It's not like I paid attention directly to it—because I didn't. But, indirectly, I heard some things.

Philippians 4:13: *I can do everything through Him who gives me strength.*

We believe that as human beings, we have limitations. However, when you put your trust and belief in Christ, anything is possible.

This is something you should feel each and every day.

Again, as a football player, if I put all of my trust solely in myself, I would surely come up short. However, by putting my faith in God in all things, I've found everything will come to pass.

That includes our faith. Our faith is something that is continuously evolving. It is a necessary constant in our lives, but one that is constantly expanding. People who have experienced faith have to keep it in their life; if they don't, they can feel the absence of it.

There are those who want to say they have faith, yet they are never satisfied with anything. They are always searching for something to fill that void created by the lack of faith. They might know what it is that they are searching for, or maybe they do not.

That's why I believe one of my duties of my faith is to share it. And let me tell you, that gives me a great sense of joy and peace. In fact, speaking to others about faith might be more of a blessing to me than to the people I'm speaking to.

Exodus 15:22—15:27: *Then Moses led Israel from the Red Sea and they went into the Desert of Shur. For three days they traveled in the desert without finding water. When they came to Marah, they could not drink its water because it was bitter (That is why the place is called Marah). So the people grumbled against Moses saying, "What are we to drink?"*

Then Moses cried out to the Lord, and the Lord showed him a piece of wood. He threw it into the water, and the water became sweet.

There the Lord made a decree and a law for them, and there He tested them. He said, "If you listen carefully to the voice of the Lord your God and do what is right in His eyes, if you pay attention to His commands and keep all His decrees, I will not bring on you any of the diseases I brought on the Egyptians, for I am the Lord, who heals you.

Then they came to Elim, where there were twelve springs and seventy palm trees, and they camped there, near the water.

This speaks to me about how our walk with Christ needs to be continuously evolving. Too often people settle for less than the whole. They settle for just a piece, instead of the whole thing. They are satisfied with the blessing they receive today and wake up with that same satisfaction tomorrow, instead of an excitement for what is ahead the coming day. You have to celebrate today, but be ready to search for tomorrow's blessing.

I can apply that to my own life. I was very blessed at Weber State during my redshirt freshman year as the starting quarterback. After that year ended, I had to be looking for the next blessing. That took me to Snow College. Yes, it was a great year at Snow. But had I given up the search and exploration there, I would have never gone on to Oklahoma and the blessings that awaited me there.

And that is why I am ready for the next challenge, wherever that might take me.

Here is the testimony I gave at church in Oklahoma City, Oklahoma, in December of 2000, the morning after we won the Big 12 Conference championship by beating Kansas State in Kansas City, Missouri:

It's an honor that my Lord and Savior has decided to bring me here and let me share with you what He's done in my life. He is awesome.

My alarm went off at 7 a.m. this morning. I was ready to hit snooze for a couple of hours.

A lot of you might be thinking I woke up with a smile because we're Big 12 champions. And I do smile because we are. But the grin that you see on my face right now is really due to the opportunity God's given me to be here to share with you. It's a blessing in my life when I get that opportunity.

It revives me in my commitment to the Lord. I'm going to give you a little bit of the story of my life.

To tell you a little bit about who I am: I come from Aberdeen, South Dakota, which is in the northeast corner of the state. It is 45 minutes from the North Dakota border and an hour from the Minnesota border. My dad is the head coach for a Division II four-year college, Northern State, which is in Aberdeen. My mother is the principal at the public high school in town. She was my principal. It made for some uneasy nights at home.

As far as I can remember, I've enjoyed the game of football. I enjoyed being around my dad and his team.

I knew at a young age that I wanted to play college football. I wanted that opportunity. And I wanted to play at a great university. I was successful in high school. But not a lot of great opportunities came my way.

When I was young—and I'll come back to this later on— and growing up, I knew the Lord, but I didn't love the Lord. And there is a fundamental difference between those two. I went to church on Sunday mornings. I went to a Catholic school until eighth grade. But I hadn't given God authority over my life.

I left high school and had the chance to go to a Division

I-AA university, Weber State, in Ogden Utah, right next to Salt Lake. It was my first time away from home.

God was not No. 1 in my life. Football was my God at that time—that's not something I'm proud of, but that's how it was. But God humbled me very quickly.

I redshirted my first year. Then, battling for a starting spot in the spring, I tore the ACL in my knee. I battled back and got some playing time the next fall, and then my coach left. While I was at Weber State, I was living for Josh Heupel. I was not living for the Lord.

While I was going on—this is how I describe it—weights were being thrown upon my shoulders, continuously day after day, more and more weight. It was crushing me. I went from a walk to a crawl to where I wasn't moving at all. I was getting crushed

I'd look at the mirror in the morning, and there wasn't a smile on the outside or on the inside. I wasn't happy with who I was, and what I was, as a person

I decided to go to a junior college, thinking—and this wasn't a smart thought process—that was the change I needed in my life, so that when I looked in the mirror every morning I'd be happy with who and what I was as a person. I thought the new challenges and new opportunities would revive my life. I thought that would make me excited and happy.

That first spring I was there at Snow, more and more weight was being placed upon my shoulders. Yet every morning, when I looked in the mirror, I was less happy with who and what I was as a person.

I still wasn't moving. I was stationary. I decided—because I knew the Lord at one time in my life and what He could do—I made the biggest decision of my life. I gave it all to God, all the authority in my life. I decided I would love God.

I decided that Josh Heupel's way wasn't going to be the way I went anymore. I was going to do what He wanted, when He wanted and how He wanted it done.

While I was at Snow, which wasn't a luxurious place—neither was Weber State, for that matter—we had 15-hour bus trips. We were cramped in there on our bus trips. And we weren't always eating well.

I lived with seven other people in an apartment. There were three guys in one room, two in each of the other two rooms, and I got a single. You think I had a good deal? Your closet at home was bigger than my room. Let me tell you; I could literally reach out sideways and touch the wall. While I was lying down, my hands could touch the wall behind me, and my feet could touch the other wall. It was cramped living quarters to say the least.

But at that time, I made a commitment to the Lord.

So I read from Deuteronomy 8:2

Remember how the Lord your God led you all the way in the desert these forty years, to humble you and test you in order to know what was in your heart, whether or not you would keep His commands. He humbled you, causing you to hunger and then feeding you with manna, which neither you nor your fathers had known, to teach you that man does not live on bread alone but on every word that comes from the mouth of the Lord. Your clothes did not wear out and your feet did not swell during these forty years. Know then in your heart that as a man disciplines his son, so the Lord your God disciplines you.

God is not going to be on your time. God has His time. He will not put you in a position that you cannot handle or where you cannot stand strong. I was blessed with a great opportunity after I recommitted myself to the Lord. It came about because of the change I made to love the Lord.

I say that I've always worked as hard as I can to be the

best football player that I can be—while I was growing up, at Weber State and at Snow and at Oklahoma. I've always given every ounce of energy I have to be the best I can be, watching film, throwing, trying to get my body in better shape—everything I could within that realm. Nothing changed in that aspect. What did change was I gave it all to the Lord.

Suddenly, I became an All-American at Snow College. I was blessed with an opportunity to fulfill a lifelong dream to play at a prestigious school with great tradition at the University of Oklahoma, where everything I need—or could possibly think of—to be successful, was in line.

What changed? Nothing I did as a person. I didn't spend any more time throwing, or doing anything different. Everything I needed was in line. The only thing that changed was having God in my life—what the Lord was doing in my life.

He won't take you to a place until you're ready to do His work, to use His platform, to glorify Him. He didn't take me to that place where I would have these opportunities until I was ready, until He had authority over my life and until I was ready to use the platform.

To be honest, I didn't want to get up this morning at 7 o'clock. But it's the platform He's given me, the blessing He's given me. Use that opportunity.

I read now from Deuteronomy 8:6.

Observe the commands of the Lord your God, walking in His ways and revering Him. For the Lord your God is bringing you into a good land—a land with streams and pools of water, with springs flowing in the valley and hills; a land with wheat and barley, vines and fig trees, pomegranates, olive oil and honey; a land where bread will not be scarce and you will lack nothing; a land where the rocks are iron and you can dig copper out of the hills.

Suddenly, great opportunities and blessings are being showered upon me faster and quicker than I can imagine.

Now, living in the blessing is not an easy thing to do. It's one of the hardest things to do. There's a scripture I go back to that maintains my strength for me, in Isaiah 54:17, *No weapon formed against you will prevail.*

Don't ever let your blessings—the things the Lord has placed in your life—become a burden. Don't let the things that the Lord has placed in your life cause you stress.

One of the names of God is Jehovah-shalom, which simply means, "He is there." When the blessing is almost becoming a burden, know that He is there.

There's a story from when I was little. I was a big Minnesota Vikings fan. They were playing in a charity basketball event in a health club that my uncle belonged to. I went to the event. I wanted to get this running back's autograph after the game. I went up to him and asked him. He said, "What do you want an autograph for? In six months, you will throw that piece of paper in the garbage." He wouldn't give me an autograph.

I was heartbroken. I admired the position he was at, and yet he wouldn't sign an autograph for me. Don't let the blessing become a burden.

I don't understand why, but sometimes now people want an autograph from me. There are times after a game when I would rather just go say hi to my family, go out to dinner with them—not be bothered and just spend time with them. My father is always there to remind me when people are asking for an autograph, 'Remember when you were a child and you wanted that autograph.' So those times when I don't want to, I am reminded to not ever let the blessing become a burden. The Lord has placed you in that position for a reason. Maybe you're supposed to share Him with that child who is asking for an autograph. Don't ever let your blessing become a burden.

I read out of Deuteronomy because it really coincides with my life. Really, it is the story of my life of sacrifice and not having everything you desire. That's where I was at while I was attending Weber State and when I got to Snow College.

Suddenly, the blessings were placed in my life.

Along the same lines as blessings is the story of Moses leading the people of Israel from the Red Sea. They traveled through the desert. There was no water. The sun was beating down upon them. I only thing that might help me relate to this experience is two-a-day practices during preseason football.

In other words, I can't fathom what was in their minds. They were doubting and complaining. But those were blessings they were given. Even though they were griping a little bit, they continued along their path to receive the full reward, the full blessing. In our Christian walk, a lot of us settle for half of the reward or a quarter of the reward, of what God wants for us. Don't ever stop your walk. Run the full race. Seek the full reward.

I could have been happy with being at junior college. That could have been the end of my race. If I would have stopped there and not sought the full reward, I wouldn't have gotten the full reward of a Big 12 championship here at Oklahoma last night. I wouldn't have gotten the reward of sharing my story of the Lord and what He's done in my life, with you today. I wouldn't get the blessing he has in store for me tomorrow morning or tomorrow afternoon. I wouldn't get the blessing of being at the Orange Bowl in January.

Wake up with an expectancy of what He has in store for you in your life. Wake up with an expectancy of what He is going to throw upon you tonight or tomorrow morning. Run the full race. Seek a full reward. Don't ever settle for anything less.

Earlier, I said how when I was younger, I knew the Lord, but I didn't love the Lord. When you love the Lord, you allow him to have complete authority over your life. He's going to do His work in you.

Deuteronomy 8:18-19 reads:

But remember the Lord your God, for it is He who gives you the ability to produce wealth, and so confirms His covenant, which He swore to your forefathers, as it is today.

If you ever forget the Lord your God and follow other gods and worship and bow down to them, I testify against you today that you will surely be destroyed. Like the nations the Lord destroyed before you, so you will be destroyed for not obeying the Lord your God.

One of the hardest things to do—it's a learning curve I've been through, and continue to go through—is when you have these blessings bestowed upon you, your first inclination as man is to veer off the path. Keep your eyes on the cross, and walk toward it—run toward it. When blessings are being showered in your life—thrown at your feet—do not look down to pick them up. They are there, and they will follow you. Run with them, and keep your eyes fixed on the cross.

That road is straight to the cross. When you look down to pick up your blessings, you will veer off that road and the devil will deceive you. All that the devil needs is a split—a small crack—to get into your life and to destroy your blessings. That will take you off the road that leads to the cross.

The other thing you have to do to continue on toward the cross and to receive your full blessing and reward is keep God involved in everything you are doing. Everything.

In the game of football, God is involved. The people on that football team—we are not undefeated. That is God's team. He is doing the mighty work in that team. You see where this team has come in two years? The only way it is possible is God's hand. Keep God involved in everything you're doing. If you keep Him involved in everything you're doing, then you know without a shadow of a doubt that you are on the right path, that you are serving Him, that He has authority over your life and that He is using you to reach others. We're all called with different blessings. The responsibilities with those blessings are all different. I've been called to speak here today. Some of you might be called to speak to someone. The impact you have on other's lives reaches further than you, as an individual, can ever imagine. It's a trickle-down affect. The one person you impact can impact a hundred. Show love to everyone. Jesus is love. Show love.

Some of you may never be called to speak. Walking down the street, you may impact someone's life. People can see Jesus in you just walking down the street. Show them that, and impact someone's life without even knowing that.

I woke up at 7 o'clock and wasn't prepared to come here as far as knowing what I was going to say. Usually I prepare well in advance. But today I just threw it together. I got in the shower and said, "Lord, today time is short. It's not of me; you're the reason I'm going there. You're calling me there. What do you want me to speak about?"

It came to me, "You're going to have an impact on people. Show them what He's done in your life, what He means to you. The impact that He's had. Let them see love. For those that do not know Him at all, may they take their first steps toward Him. For those who are walking, may they take stronger steps. May they start running toward the cross."

There's a card here that says, "How to experience new life in Christ." And there are six different descriptions and verses. Here's the simplest, and my favorite. I guess simply and favorite coincide for me:

"This is God's promise to you. If you accept Jesus, He will accept you."

I pray that those of you who have not accepted Him will accept Him. When you accept Him, it is amazing the love He has for you. He wishes to shower you with blessings more abundantly than you can imagine. He's doing that in my life. I know He's doing that in a lot of people's lives that are out there right now. The hope is that He'll do it in everyone's lives. Accept Him, and He will accept you. Show love. Continue your walk with Him. Run toward the cross. Be excited about what He's going to do in your life, an hour from now or tomorrow. Keep your eyes on the cross. Don't ever let your blessings become a burden. And show love.

Thank you. God bless you all. Wait for His blessings to be showered upon you.

That day was truly a blessing because I was able to share my testimony with the people in church that day, and with those of you reading this right now.

There's no doubt the most important gift you can give your kids is faith. Put them in a setting where God is number one in the household. That's the way it was for my family. Being a kid on Sunday mornings, I would play sick sometime so I could watch NFL Countdown on ESPN. Thankfully, though, my parents had God in our household, and I had that strong foundation of faith my parents built for us.

Because there comes a point in life where no longer is it the parents' decision for God to be number one in their kids' lives—the young person has to make a decision. And that is that God is going to be the most important part of his or her life. That doesn't happen right away for everyone. When you are raised in a Christian home, no matter what happens in a kid's life, he or she will come back to that foundation of faith.

Only the peace and joy that comes from that relationship with God will satisfy someone completely. If they have a taste of that early in their life at home, they may try different avenues as they grow up. Eventually though, they will come back to that relationship with God.

I came upon a point when I was tired of trying it my own way. I thought, "Okay, I've tried it my way. Now I need to give God's way a shot."

When I did, I completely enjoyed who and what I saw in the mirror when I woke up in the morning. I enjoyed life a lot more.

Is Jesus Christ your savior? That's what you're going to be judged on. We are not here to judge others. That is one of the biggest mistakes Christians make, judging others. Just accept His gift of love. Then tell others about this gift.

12

Young People's Challenge

To hear some of the stories about what kids are doing today is scary. These young people are not equipped to understand the full consequence of their actions. That's where character comes in and what kids learn from their family and friends.

Some people display character only when they're around others. For some people, displaying or talking about character is important to them. It is easy to do the things that are right when people are watching. But how do you respond to a situation when no one else is watching? That is when true character rises to the surface.

At a young age, family does play an integral part in decision-making. Children's behavior is a reflection of the behavior they see being modeled before them.

I believe it's important that people get their kids involved in anything and everything, so as much time as possible is spent in a constructive way. They will learn many of life's lessons through those endeavors. More importantly, they will have a focus that will keep their attention off destructive behavior.

At a young age, I wrote down what I was going to do each day. I was not allowed to sit at home all summer or hang out with my friends playing video games. My parents had no problem with me spending time with my friends, but it had to be something constructive and active.

Any place is what you make it to be; no more or no less. That being said, I really enjoyed growing up in Aberdeen. We always focused on enjoying what we had, and not worrying about what we didn't have.

There were a lot of opportunities for me as a kid. My parents or babysitters were always willing to take me to basketball camps. What I enjoyed the most when I was younger, was Friday afternoons, getting ready with my dad for his team's football games. Those are some of my best memories.

I remember how competitive my dad was. As a coach, if you win, it's a good night. If not, it was a long week ahead of us. When he came home, you always knew what kind of day it had been. Some people say there are two types of women, coaches' wives and non-coaches' wives. You have to be a special woman, there's no doubt, to be married to a coach.

My mother is the most compassionate, genuinely caring person I ever met. That's why she's in the field that she's in because she genuinely cares about kids. She's a leader, the strongest woman I've ever met. I'll never forget sitting on our fireplace after hockey practice, my mom taking care of me. She was always there, the person who was never late picking me up or dropping me off. I could set my watch by her.

My father never said, "Josh, you're going to be an athlete." Athletics is something I always enjoyed. I also liked working on the farm with him. Hard work is the backbone of our family. That's something my father was always looking to get across to me. I didn't know, like he did, what it was like to pick rocks or throw hay bales all day long.

So in action or words, my father always reminded me of what hard work was, from seeing him work as a coach to the times on the farm in South Dakota.

When young people are ready to tackle a great endeavor, they have to be ready to sacrifice certain things and make a commitment to the task at hand. In my case, I've found that people rarely understand the time commitment that is involved with being a student-athlete at the major university level. One of the greatest skills these athletes learn is time management, being able to find a balance and keep it.

That's the most important thing. Work as hard as you possible can, do a little more, do a little extra, and then call it a day.

Too often, kids today envision an end result, and do little or nothing to reach that. For myself, I needed a long-term goal and had to have short-term and intermediate goals. That's why I have daily, weekly, monthly and yearly goals that I can look at and chart the progress.

That's part of sports, being confident in what you're doing, knowing that you are giving everything you have each and every day, but that you are doing that along the correct path, one that allows you to reach the end result. Too often, people get sidetracked. They don't have things right in front of them. Things can take you off the road to success if you are not focused or committed.

Kids need to learn and be taught that no matter where they go, they have to earn their position, in sports and in life.

It comes down often to how you react when you are confronted with an adversity. Kids either crawl off to a corner or they rise up to the challenge. People would be surprised by how much they can accomplish when they set their mind to something. Today, all too often, people set limitations on who and what they can become. If they shoot for the moon, they may end up there. Or they may end up somewhere near there, among stars.

We constantly measure ourselves against others, or other

teams and companies. But it comes back to the fact that we are always competing against ourselves, which puts winning and losing in context. We focus on performing at the highest level we can. That's when we will be the most successful. Athletics are a great learning environment for life. Every situation we face on the field can be equated to life. All of the skills that are needed to be successful as an athlete should be directly translated to our lives.

You can make the best or worst out of anything. Was it going to be fun at Snow, or enjoyable? Well, one look at the surroundings could have someone focus on what wasn't there. But you have to focus on what is there. Is your glass half empty or half full? Mine is always half full.

Josh prepares to launch the OU air attack.

Josh balances his Vikings helmet at ten months.

Josh at age one and a half years.

Josh at age five with his new lockers from Santa.

Josh at age five playing hockey in Aberdeen.

Josh, age six, on the practice field with his dad.

Joshua showing off his muscles to sister Andrea.

Josh at age nine with his basketball.

Josh takes a shot during his sophomore year of high school for the Aberdeen Eagles.

Josh poses for his team picture as a senior in 1996.

Josh at Weber State University.

Josh (far lower right) with all the Heupel family in 1995.

Josh (far lower right) with his mother's family (Kelly).

Josh fishing in Oklahoma, Easter 1999.

Josh with friends Josh Norman and Julie McGehee at OU Fellowship of Christian Athletes meeting.

Josh on the sidelines during an OU football game.

Family photo at Senior Day: Ken, Josh, Andrea and Cindy.

Josh calls the signals during the Texas Tech game.

Josh looks for a receiver downfield.

Josh delivers a pass during the Sooners' national championship season.

Josh scrambles out of the pocket for a first down.

Josh looks for a receiver near the OU sideline.

Josh finds the end zone—only this time on the ground.

13

A Season for the Ages

Game 1

OU 55, UTEP 14
Sooners Maul Miners

NORMAN, Oklahoma, (Sept. 2, 2000) – So much preseason hype had been given to so many teams around the country.

Except the Oklahoma Sooners, who were ranked Number 19 in the nation.

"This football team never looked at preseason rankings," OU quarterback Josh Heupel said "We watched very little of the media picks in the preseason. We did see–or hear about, at least–a Big 12 preview, in which Kansas State and Nebraska were mentioned. A group of players in our training room were watching that."

The players looked at each other, eyebrows raised.

"We said at that point," Heupel said, "that we were going to shock the world. Our entire football team believed we were going to win and be successful and play for a national title. I know I did. I truly believed that I would, or that we'd have every opportunity to do so. We knew that if we prepared ourselves, we'd have a great chance to be successful."

In the fall workouts, some closed-door soul-searching revealed OU's players to be on the same page.

"Our seniors got up and talked during two-a-days about expectations for the season and how we were going to meet them," Heupel said.

Yet the seed had been planted well before that. The Sooners came off the 1999 season with a 7-5 record.

"That's part of what drove this football team during the off-season," Heupel said. "Our confidence came from the fact we had some success the year before. But we hadn't learn how to win and hadn't paid the total price. During the off-season and preseason, we paid the price."

And it was UTEP that paid the price in the opener.

"The week of the UTEP game, we were getting so tired of beating up on each other that we were in desperate need of playing another team," Heupel said.

The Sooners knew there were a lot bigger games down the road. But to OU, no game was bigger than the one that was next.

Yet there were butterflies in the stomach as the 2000 season kicked off.

"Heading into the first game, it's always the same," Heupel said. "There is a nervous tension building. All the effort and energy is about to pay dividends. It's the first opportunity we have to show who and what we are as a football team. We were a very confident football team."

Boosting that confidence was the home opener.

"There's nothing like Opening Day at the University of Oklahoma, where the people are waiting impatiently for the season to begin," Heupel said.

The temperature was 106 degrees.

"I remember looking up in the stands, and everyone was fanning themselves," Heupel said. "It was hot as heck, just roasting."

OU was hot on the field as well, putting up 55 points.

"You're never playing against the scoreboard; you're playing against yourself," Heupel said. "At halftime, we talked about the things we needed to improve on in the second half."

Though the offensive output was impressive–409 yards of total offense–the Sooners saw where they could have done a lot of things better.

"We knew after that game that as an offense, we needed to improve on our execution," Heupel said. "We also discovered that we had the opportunity to be a great football team."

That belief, in part, was due to a fast, hard-hitting defense. "We believed our defense would become great as the season went on," Heupel said.

Score by quarters

UTEP Miners	7	0	7	0 - 14	**Record: (0-1)**	
Oklahoma Sooners ...	17	10	7	21 - 55	**Record: (1-0)**	

Scoring summary:

First quarter
13:41 OU - Heupel, Josh 1 yd run (Duncan, Tim kick), 3 plays, 17 yards, TOP 0:50, UTEP 0 - OU 7

04:48 UTEP - Tessier,P. 6 yd pass from Perez,R. (Bishop,R. kick), 6 plays, 62 yards, TOP 2:32, UTEP 7 - OU 7

02:55 OU - Smith, Trent 4 yd pass from Heupel, Josh (Duncan, Tim kick), 5 plays, 46 yards, TOP 1:53, UTEP 7 - OU 14

00:00 OU - Duncan, Tim 22 yd field goal, 6 plays, 53 yards, TOP 1:38, UTEP 7 - OU 17

Second quarter
11:05 OU - Williams, Roy 35 yd interception return (Duncan, Tim kick), UTEP 7 - OU 24

00:18 OU - Duncan, Tim 22 yd field goal, 10 plays, 47 yards, TOP 2:57, UTEP 7 - OU 27

Third quarter
14:31 OU - Savage, Antwone 31 yd pass from Heupel, Josh (Duncan, Tim kick), 1 play, 31 yards, TOP 0:07, UTEP 7 - OU 34

04:27 UTEP - Porter,C. 19 yd run (Bishop,R. kick), 5 plays, 37 yards, TOP 1:26, UTEP 14 - OU 34

Fourth quarter
09:22 OU - Works, Renaldo 19 yd run (Duncan, Tim kick), 5 plays, 77 yards, TOP 1:12, UTEP 14 - OU 41

07:54 OU - Works, Renaldo 6 yd run (Duncan, Tim kick), 2 plays, 12 yards, TOP 0:39, UTEP 14 - OU 48

04:05 OU - Works, Renaldo 5 yd run (Duncan, Tim kick), 9 plays, 31 yards, TOP 3:14, UTEP 14 - OU 55

	UTEP	OU
FIRST DOWNS	19	18
RUSHES-YARDS (NET)	38-125	33-122
PASSING YDS (NET)	217	287
Passes Att-Comp-Int	42-21-2	39-19-1
TOTAL OFFENSE PLAYS-YARDS	80-342	72-409
Fumble Returns-Yards	0-0	2-34
Punt Returns-Yards	4-8	4-31
Kickoff Returns-Yards	5-70	1-3
Interception Returns-Yards	1-23	2-41
Punts (Number-Avg)	8-41.8	7-42.6
Fumbles-Lost	6-5	3-2
Penalties-Yards	7-67	9-70
Possession Time	33:11	26:49
Sacks By: Number-Yards	1-10	0-0

RUSHING: UTEP Miners-Porter,C. 11-79; Sanchez,J. 4-13; Cleveland,R. 7-13; Austin,S. 5-9; Phillips,W. 1-9; Natkin,B. 1-6; Perez,R. 7-0; Lunnon,G. 1-minus 2; Mays,L. 1-minus 2. Oklahoma Sooners-Works, Renaldo 19-98; Griffin, Q. 9-28; Littrell, Seth 1-1; Burcham, Bubba 1-minus 2; Heupel, Josh 3-minus 3.

PASSING: UTEP Miners-Perez,R. 18-37-2-197; Phillips,W. 3-5-0-20. Oklahoma Sooners-Heupel, Josh 18-36-1-274; Hybl, Nate 1-3-0-13.

RECEIVING: UTEP Miners-Mays,L. 5-58; Natkin,B. 5-43; Ray,A. 4-65; Knapp,J. 4-40; Tessier,P. 1-6; Porter,C. 1-4; Austin,S. 1-1. Oklahoma Sooners-Savage, Antwone 5-87; Mackey, Damian 3-54; Works, Renaldo 3-24; Griffin, Q. 2-48; Norman, Josh 2-43; Woolfolk, Andre 1-13; Steenhoek, E. 1-13; Smith, Trent 1-4; Littrell, Seth 1-1.

INTERCEPTIONS: UTEP Miners-Young,J. 1-23. Oklahoma Sooners-Williams, Roy 1-35; Thatcher, J.T. 1-6.

Stadium: Memorial Stadium. Attendance: 74,761; Kickoff time: 6:38. End of Game: 10:10 p.m. Total elapsed time: 3:32; Officials: Referee: Tom Walker; Umpire: Joe Darden; Linesman: Tim Crowley; Line judge: Ron Underwood; Back judge: Scott Koch; Field judge: Duane Osborne; Side judge: Ron Murphy. Temperature: 106. Wind: S-10 mph Weather: Partly Cloudy

SACKS (UA-A): UTEP Miners-Holloway,M. 1-0. Oklahoma Sooners-None.

TACKLES (UA-A): UTEP Miners-Merkens,T. 6-2; Wiseman,B. 4-1; Sheppard,A.J. 4-1; Holloway,M. 3-2; Walker,D. 2-3; Williams,G. 3-0; Cooks,W. 3-0; Clemons,C. 3-0; Young,J. 2-1; Fette,R. 2-1; Smith,P. 2-1; Woodard,T. 2-0; High,K. 1-1; Walker,D.J. 1-1; Kerr,D. 1-1; King,Ba. 0-2; Dorenbos,J. 0-2; Clarke,S. 1-0; Natkin,B. 1-0; Robertson,J. 0-1. Oklahoma Sooners-Thatcher, J.T. 8-3; Calmus, Rocky 5-5; Steffen, Roger 5-5; Jones, Ontei 5-4; Thompson, M. 3-3; Williams, Roy 4-0; Heinecke, Cory 4-0; Klein, Kory 3-1; Strait, Derrick 1-2; Thunander, Eric 2-0; Littrell, Seth 1-1; Babb, Brandon 1-1; Richardson, R. 0-2; Fisher, Ryan 0-2; Cody, Dan 0-2; Wilson-Guest, J 1-0; Jackson, Brent 1-0; Donley, Lance 1-0; Burcham, Bubba 1-0; Callens, Corey 0-1; McCoy, Matt 0-1.

GAME NOTES:

–Oklahoma's 55 points tonight were its most since beating Missouri 55-17 on Nov. 7, 1992, under Head Coach Gary Gibbs.

–The game time temperature of 106 degrees broke the previous Memorial Stadium record high of 105 degrees (vs. North Texas in 1998).

–Derrick Strait and Kory Klein, both redshirt freshmen, made their first career starts on defense, while sophomore Mike Skinner made his first career start on the offensive line.

–UTEP's first-quarter touchdown was the first touchdown allowed by the Sooner defense at home since the second quarter of last year's game against Texas A&M. The scoreless span lasted a total of 10 quarters.

–Senior free safety J.T. Thatcher made his first career start on defense for the Sooners and recorded his first career interception. His only other career start was as a tailback in 1997 against Nebraska.

–Sophomore Roy Williams' 35-yard interception for a touchdown was his third interception in his last seven regular-season games.

–Williams' interception marked the second time in the last two regular-season games that OU recorded an interception for a touchdown (Mike Woods returned a 44-yard interception for a touchdown last year against Oklahoma State).

–Andre Woolfolk played wide receiver and cornerback. He became the first Sooner to play both offense and defense in the same game since Steve Zabel in 1969. Woolfolk played a significant defensive role in the second half as he took part in 31 plays as a cornerback after halftime.

–Tonight's attendance of 74,761 was the largest in a season-opening game since 1988.

–The crowd marked the third largest in Memorial Stadium's current configuration.

–UTEP accomplished what no team could last season by scoring 14 points against the Sooners at Memorial Stadium. Baylor's 10 points last year were the most recorded by an OU opponent in Norman.

–True freshman Renaldo Works scored his first three career touchdowns on runs of 19, six, and five yards. The last time a true freshman scored at least two rushing touchdowns was in 1993 (Jerald Moore against SMU).

–Works' three-touchdown performance was the first by an OU running back since De'Mond Parker in 1996 against Nebraska. Both Works and Parker attended Booker T. Washington High School in Tulsa.

–OU's win tonight extended its home winning streak to eight games. It's the longest home winning streak since the 1985-88 seasons when the Sooners reeled off 19 consecutive home victories.

–Heupel threw for 274 yards. He has thrown for at least 200 yards in 11 of his 13 games at Oklahoma.

–Five true freshmen played for OU tonight: Dan Cody, Lance Donley, Teddy Lehman, Jimmy Wilkerson and Renaldo Works.

Game 2

OU 45, Arkansas State 7
Oklahoma Throttles Arkansas State

NORMAN, Oklahoma, (Sept. 9, 2000) – Oklahoma put up 28 first-half points and the defense allowed Arkansas State only a second-quarter touchdown as the Sooners improved to 2-0.

"A football team makes its biggest improvement between the first and second week of the season," quarterback Josh Heupel said, "because you have something to go on after that first game. We had a game film under our belt. Once you get the first game underneath you, you start to, as a team, form an identity."

Though Oklahoma was starting to get a little attention, it realized a slip-up would dash all of its dreams.

"We talked again, before the game, about how on any given Saturday that anyone can beat anyone else," Heupel said. "Do I believe that cliché? Yes, because it's early in the season and anything can happen. We knew that as a football team, we had to improve week to week to meet our goals. And we had another great crowd in Norman."

The Sooners cruised to 533 yards of total offense, including 325 through the air. Eleven Oklahoma receivers caught passes.

"Offensively, we were able to spread the ball around," Heupel said. "Our offense is predicated on finding the open receiver."

The defense dominated as was expected. The Sooner special teams also sparkled, led by J.T. Thatcher's 66-yard punt return for a touchdown. The Sooners' only punt went for 66 yards.

"Our special teams were shining again," Heupel said. "Special teams are a key component to our success. On offense and defense, our special teams helped us out with field position."

For the second game in a row, Heupel started the scoring with a quarterback sneak.

"That began my early season streak as the best quarterback sneak guy in the nation," Heupel joked.

The Sooners actually had dropped from No. 19 to No. 20 in the week between the opener and the Arkansas State game.

"This football team never once cared about its ranking," Heupel said. "We knew if we took care of business that our end result would be what we wanted it to be. Nobody is noticing us at that point. But we knew in a few weeks, we'd be in the spotlight with the opportunity to shine."

Score by quarters

Arkansas State 0	7	0	0	- 7	**Record: (0-2)**	
Oklahoma Sooners ...14	14	7	10	- 45	**Record: (2-0)**	

Scoring summary:
First quarter
09:25 OU - Heupel, Josh 1 yd run (Duncan, Tim kick), 15-80 5:35, ASU 0 - OU 7

03:37 OU - Thatcher, J.T. 66 yd punt return (Duncan, Tim kick), ASU 0 - OU 14

Second quarter

14:55 OU - Mackey, Damian 26 yd pass from Heupel, Josh (Duncan, Tim kick), 6-42 2:04, ASU 0 - OU 21

08:29 OU - Woolfolk, Andre 19 yd pass from Heupel, Josh (Duncan, Tim kick), 4-41 1:33, ASU 0 - OU 28

04:41 ASU - Danny Smith 33 yd run (Nick Gatto kick), 7-80 3:48, ASU 7 - OU 28

Third quarter

11:48 OU - Woolfolk, Andre 35 yd pass from Heupel, Josh (Duncan, Tim kick), 5-49 2:06, ASU 7 - OU 35

Fourth quarter

11:45 OU - Works, Renaldo 75 yd run (Duncan, Tim kick), 1-75 0:14, ASU 7 - OU 42

04:46 OU - Duncan, Tim 26 yd field goal, 10-28 4:33, ASU 7 - OU 45

	ASU	OU
FIRST DOWNS	10	23
RUSHES-YARDS (NET)	21-84	35-208
PASSING YDS (NET)	191	325
Passes Att-Comp-Int	33-21-1	34-26-1
TOTAL OFFENSE PLAYS-YARDS	54-275	69-533
Fumble Returns-Yards	0-0	0-0
Punt Returns-Yards.	0-0	5-160
Kickoff Returns-Yards	4-89	2-20
Interception Returns-Yards	1-0	1-2
Punts (Number-Avg)	9-42.7	1-66.0
Fumbles-Lost	1-0	0-0
Penalties-Yards	14-97	11-95
Possession Time	30:39	29:21
Sacks By: Number-Yards	0-0	0-0

RUSHING: Arkansas State-Danny Smith 4-47; Jonathan Adams 12-43; Jacquis Walker 3-2; Cleo Lemon 2-minus 8. Oklahoma Sooners-Works, Renaldo 12-109; Griffin, Q. 13-58; Littrell, Seth 3-14; Heupel, Josh 5-12; Norman, Josh 1-8; Fagan, Curtis 1-7.

PASSING: Arkansas State-Cleo Lemon 20-31-1-183; Andy Shatley 1-2-0-8. Oklahoma Sooners-Heupel, Josh 24-32-1-301; Hybl, Nate 2-2-0-24.

RECEIVING: Arkansas State-Robert Kilow 10-108; J. Hickenbotham 4-20; Jacquis Walker 3-15; Mark Hamilton 2-32; Alvin Powell 1-11; Danny Smith 1-5. Oklahoma Sooners-Woolfolk, Andre 5-102; Savage, Antwone 4-47; Smith, Trent 3-34; Griffin, Q. 3-24; Norman, Josh 3-minus 1; Mackey, Damian 2-38; Works, Renaldo 2-12; Fagan, Curtis 1-34; Steenhoek, E. 1-16; Donley, Lance 1-11; Hess, Jeremy 1-8.

INTERCEPTIONS: Arkansas State-Hanis Bowens 1-0. Oklahoma Sooners-Thatcher, J.T. 1-2.

FUMBLES: Arkansas State-Cleo Lemon 1-0. Oklahoma Sooners-None.

Stadium: Memorial Stadium; Attendance: 74,730; Kickoff time: 6:38 pm; End of Game: 9:45 pm; Total elapsed time: 3:07; Officials: Referee: W. Davenport; Umpire: JC Leimbach; Linesman: Don Kapral; Line judge: Gary Brown; Back judge: Ron Murphy; Field judge: Rick Skaggs; Side judge: Phil Laurie; Temperature: 92; Wind: S-SE 20; Weather: Mostly Clear

SACKS (UA-A): Arkansas State-None. Oklahoma Sooners-None.

TACKLES (UA-A): Arkansas State-Charles Mabry 5-4; Joe Jones 3-5; Quincy Williams 4-2; Segun Ajigbeda 5-0; Les Echols 3-2; Hanis Bowens 2-3; Russell Seaton 2-2; Erik Kellim 3-0; John Bradley 1-2; Tyshon Reed 1-2; Chris Hogan 1-2; Kevin Woods 2-0; Maci Davis 2-0; Lenny Johnson 2-0; Brandon Rager 2-0; J.C. Miller 2-0; Bobby Patterson 1-1; Chris Jackson 1-1; Sean Mitchell 0-2; Corey Williams 1-0; Andy Shatley 1-0; Kishan Cotton 1-0; Maurice Joyner 0-1; James Morman 0-1. Oklahoma Sooners-Marshall, T. 6-6; Thatcher, J.T. 2-4; Strait, Derrick 2-4; Williams, Roy 3-2; Jones, Ontei 2-2; Thompson, M. 2-2; Everage, B. 2-2; Holleyman, Bary 1-3; Cody, Dan 0-4; Calmus, Rocky 2-1; Steffen, Roger 1-1; Heinecke, Cory 0-2; Fisher, Ryan 0-2; Wilson-Guest, J 1-0; McCoy, Matt 1-0; Duncan, Tim 1-0; Richardson, R. 0-1; Klein, Kory 0-1.

GAME NOTES:

–J.T Thatcher's first-quarter 66-yard punt return for a touchdown was not only his second career return for a touchdown, but his third return of more than 50 yards (also recorded returns last year of 52 yards vs. Baylor and 81 yards for a touchdown vs. Oklahoma State).

–Thatcher's third-quarter interception was his second of the season.

–Tonight's crowd of 74,730 marked OU's seventh consecutive home sell-out.

–Sooners seeing their first action of the season tonight were redshirt-freshman Brandon Everage, junior Barry Holleyman and starting senior linebacker Torrance Marshall.

–Thatcher's 160 punt-return yards (on five returns) broke the school record set last year by Jarrail Jackson against Missouri when he had six returns for 146 yards. The 160 punt-return yards were also the most ever recorded against an Arkansas State team.

–Josh Heupel's three touchdown passes tonight upped his career total to 35, tying Cale Gundy's record. It has taken Heupel only 13 regular-season games to reach 35, while it took Gundy 40 regular-season contests.

–Jeff Ferguson's 66-yard punt in the third quarter with 3:30 remaining was the Sooners' first punt of the evening. The 66-yard boomer was the third longest of his career. He also booted a 57-yard punt against UTEP last Saturday.

–Andre Woolfolk's five catches for 102 yards receiving and two touchdowns marked personal career highs in all three categories. It also marked the 44th time in OU history that a Sooner went over the century mark in a game.

–The 75-yard fourth-quarter touchdown run by Renaldo Works was not the longest by an OU true-freshman. That record is held by Marcus Dupree, who made an 86-yard touchdown run against Nebraska in 1982.

–Heupel's 313 yards of total offense against Arkansas State moved him into seventh place on the all-time Sooner list, moving him ahead of Heisman Trophy winners Billy Sims (3,813) and Steve Owens (3,925). Heupel has recorded 3,946 career yards of total offense.

–The Sooners' point total in this season's first two games (100) is the most earned in any two opening OU games since 1989 (73 vs. New Mexico State and 33 vs. Baylor for a total of 106).

–Tonight's game marked the second time in OU history that the team has produced a 300-yard passer, a 100-yard rusher and a 100-yard receiver. Heupel threw for 301 yards, Works ran for 109 yards and Woolfolk racked up 102 receiving yards. Cale Gundy threw for 324 yards versus Virginia in the 1991 Gator Bowl while Mike Gaddis ran for 104 yards and Corey Warren tallied 110 receiving yards.

–Woolfolk participated in 37 offensive plays tonight, seven special teams plays and five defensive plays.

Game 3

OU 42, Rice 14
Sooners Spot, Destroy Owls

NORMAN, Oklahoma, (Sept. 23, 2000) – Number 19 Oklahoma made short work of Rice, taking an early lead and allowing the Owls only six points in the first half and eight in the second.

"We had a bye week the week before, so we were trying to fix things within our own football team that needed to be done," OU quarterback Josh Heupel said. "We didn't come out and play great right away. We weren't executing."

However, things started to click.

Quentin Griffin ran for 117 yards and three touchdowns for the Sooners. On defense, Rocky Calmus had 14 tackles and Torrance Marshall added 11.

"It was a game where, offensively, we didn't feel like we played up to our potential," Heupel said. "We felt we could execute at a higher level of efficiency. It was kind of like we were happy to get the first part of our season over and get down to the real business at hand, which was the conference opener the next week against Kansas."

Also, the Sooners welcomed back members of the 1985 national championship Oklahoma team.

"They were all gracious. It was great to have those guys back, and I was able to meet a lot of them," Heupel said. "Brian Bosworth talked to me after the game. He said, 'You have to be a leader and get everyone to be confident. You have to have a swagger of expecting a victory when you walk down that ramp in two weeks against Texas.' We did."

Score by quarters

Rice 6   0   8   0 - 14   **Record: (1-3, 0-1)**

Oklahoma 14   7   14   7 - 42   **Record: (3-0)**

Scoring summary:

First quarter

10:44 OU - Griffin, Q. 2 yd run (Duncan, Tim kick), 6 plays, 54 yards, TOP 2:20, RICE 0 - OU 7

06:00 RICE - Webber 29 yd pass from Wulf (Crabtree kick failed), 10 plays, 80 yards, TOP 4:44, RICE 6 - OU 7

03:35 OU - Griffin, Q. 3 yd run (Duncan, Tim kick), 7 plays, 50 yards, TOP 2:25, RICE 6 - OU 14

Second quarter

01:08 OU - Heupel, Josh 1 yd run (Duncan, Tim kick), 9 plays, 60 yards, TOP 3:55, RICE 6 - OU 21

Third quarter

07:47 RICE - Evans 4 yd run (Hawkins pass), 9 plays, 75 yards, TOP 4:31, RICE 14 - OU 21

03:13 OU - Griffin, Q. 21 yd run (Duncan, Tim kick), 7 plays, 80 yards, TOP 1:47, RICE 14 - OU 28

00:15 OU - Norman, Josh 4 yd pass from Heupel, Josh (Duncan, Tim kick), 3 plays, 57 yards, TOP 1:11, RICE 14 - OU 35

Fourth quarter

05:46 OU - Works, Renaldo 6 yd pass from Heupel, Josh (Duncan, Tim kick), 6 plays, 48 yards, TOP 2:33, RICE 14 - OU 42

	RICE	OU
FIRST DOWNS 14		24
RUSHES-YARDS (NET) 51-145		33-189
PASSING YDS (NET) 117		343
Passes Att-Comp-Int 12-6-1		36-28-2
TOTAL OFFENSE PLAYS-YARDS . . .63-262		69-532
Fumble Returns-Yards 0-0		0-0
Punt Returns-Yards 2-15		4-40
Kickoff Returns-Yards 4-48		2-57

Interception Returns-Yards 2-4	1-0	
Punts (Number-Avg) 7-42.4	2-44.5	
Fumbles-Lost 6-1	1-1	
Penalties-Yards 5-36	4-25	
Possession Time 32:11	27:49	
Sacks By: Number-Yards 2-16	2-14	

RUSHING: Rice-Evans 12-55; Sadler 7-30; S.White 7-25; Tyler 8-19; Wulf 15-10; Beck 1-4; Griffin 1-2. Oklahoma Sooners-Griffin, Q. 14-117; Works, Renaldo 13-47; Heupel, Josh 5-14; Littrell, Seth 1-11.

PASSING: Rice-Wulf 6-12-1-117. Oklahoma Sooners-Heupel, Josh 27-35-2-324; Hybl, Nate 1-1-0-19.

RECEIVING: Rice-Webber 2-40; Okoronkwo 2-25; Sadler 1-41; S.White 1-11. Oklahoma Sooners-Savage, Antwone 6-63; Smith, Trent 4-50; Woolfolk, Andre 3-57; Fagan, Curtis 3-48; Griffin, Q. 3-11; Mackey, Damian 2-35; Norman, Josh 2-33; Littrell, Seth 2-16; Works, Renaldo 2-11; Donley, Lance 1-19.

INTERCEPTIONS: Rice-Gatlin 1-4; McMillan 1-0. Oklahoma Sooners-Everage, B. 1-0.

Stadium: Memorial Stadium. Attendance: 74,794; Kickoff time: 11:38 am End of Game: 2:41 pm   Total elapsed time: 3:03 p.m.; Officials: Referee: John Laurie; Umpire: R. Whittenburg; Linesman: Tim Pringle; Line judge: Mike Liner; Back judge: Mark Johnson; Field judge: Greg Burks; Side judge: M. Weatherford; Temperature: 67; Wind: NW-22mph Weather: Clear, Cool

SACKS (UA-A): Rice-Forguson 1-0; Johnson 1-0. Oklahoma Sooners-Callens, Corey 1-0; Cody, Dan 1-0; Strait, Derrick 1-0.

TACKLES (UA-A): Rice-Dendy 5-2; Hebert 4-3; Brown 5-1; Dawson 4-2; K.Smith 2-3; J.Thompson 2-3; B.Green 2-2; Shell 2-2; Ortega 2-2; Pittman 1-3; Redmon 1-2; J.White 1-2; Gatlin 2-0; Huffman 2-0; Johnson 2-0; Forguson 1-1; Chism 1-1; Engler 1-1; Jackson 0-2; Pontbriand 1-0; McMillan 1-0; Boyd 1-0; Vanover 1-0; Holmes 1-0; Erwin 1-0; Sabula 1-0; Allison 0-1. Oklahoma Sooners-Calmus, Rocky 5-9; Marshall, T. 4-7; Thompson, M. 4-4; Williams, Roy 4-2; Everage, B. 5-0; Strait, Derrick 2-3; Steffen, Roger 2-2; Fisher, Ryan 2-1; Lehman, Teddy 2-1; Littrell, Seth 1-1; Heinecke, Cory 1-1; Richardson, R. 1-1; Jones, Ontei 0-2; Thatcher, J.T. 0-2; Mackey, Damian 1-0; Cody, Dan 1-0; Callens, Corey 1-0; Klein, Kory 1-0; Donley, Lance 0-1; Smith, Trent 0-1.

Game 4

OU 34, Kansas 16
Second Half Dooms KU, Boosts OU

NORMAN, Oklahoma, (Sept. 30, 2000) – Kansas had a first-quarter lead over No. 14 Oklahoma. But after falling behind 16-10 early in the second quarter, the Sooners hit overdrive and reeled off 24 unanswered points to stay undefeated.

"Kansas is a very talented football team," Sooner quarterback Josh Heupel said. "This was serious business. We had to play well to win. But we didn't come out strong in the first quarter."

The Jayhawks also had a lot on the line.

"They pinpointed this game as one that they had to win to propel them through the season, hoping that would lead to a bowl bid," Heupel said.

The OU defense also answered the bell, holding the upset-minded Jayhawks scoreless in the second half.

Heupel completed 29 of 43 passes for 346 yards. Josh Norman had five catches for 98 yards, and Andre Woolfolk and Damian Mackey had five catches apiece.

"Everyone saw a glimpse of what this team was made of," Heupel said, "because even when we were down, we were poised and confident."

The offensive slip-ups early were a concern.

"We were stubbing our toes on offense–a lot of turnovers in their territory when we were ready to score," Heuepl said.

Heupel also made the highlights for something else, a block on a reverse for Antwone Savage's touchdown run.

"I talked all week leading up to the game about making the block on that play," Heupel said with a smile. "That was the highlight of my career. I had more people come up to me on the sidelines after that block than I ever did after a touchdown pass. And I have to admit, I watched the replay on the big-screen, too."

Coach Bob Stoops was very business-like as usual after the game.

"It was a great start to our Big 12 season," Stoops said. "Everybody get ready for the next week."

Because the coming game was against Texas.

"The Texas game was the most anticipated game of the season to that point," Heupel said. "I think it's one of the top three rival games in all of college football."

Score by quarters

Kansas Jayhawks 13   3   0   0 - 16   **Record: (2-2, 0-1)**

Oklahoma Sooners . . .10   14   10   0 - 34   **Record: (4-0, 1-0)**

Scoring summary:

First quarter

12:15 OU - Duncan, Tim 37 yd field goal, 4-6 1:24, KU 0 - OU 3

11:23 KU - Ross, Roger 77 yd pass from Smith, Dylen (Garcia, Joe kick failed), 2-80 0:52, KU 6 - OU 3

06:38 OU - Heupel, Josh 1 yd run (Duncan, Tim kick), 12-80 4:45, KU 6 - OU 10

03:05 KU - Winbush, David 29 yd run (Garcia, Joe kick), 3-52 0:18, KU 13 - OU 10

Second quarter

11:15 KU - Garcia, Joe 49 yd field goal, 12-62 5:12, KU 16 - OU 10

07:00 OU - Griffin, Q. 13 yd run (Duncan, Tim kick), 8-82 2:32, KU 16 - OU 17

02:50 OU - Savage, Antwone 40 yd run (Duncan, Tim kick), 3-51 1:01, KU 16 - OU 24

Third quarter

08:06 OU - Duncan, Tim 39 yd field goal, 6-45 2:36, KU 16 - OU 27

03:59 OU - Woolfolk, Andre 22 yd pass from Heupel, Josh (Duncan, Tim kick), 3-61 0:35, KU 16 - OU 34

	KU	OU
FIRST DOWNS 18		22
RUSHES-YARDS (NET) 45-119		28-98
PASSING YDS (NET) 258		346
Passes Att-Comp-Int 29-12-5		43-29-0

TOTAL OFFENSE PLAYS-YARDS . . .74-377	71-444	
Fumble Returns-Yards 0-0	0-0	
Punt Returns-Yards .2–2	2-21	
Kickoff Returns-Yards 2-34	3-66	
Interception Returns-Yards 0-0	5-9	
Punts (Number-Avg) 5-36.0	6-48.3	
Fumbles-Lost 3-2	5-2	
Penalties-Yards 5-38	9-78	
Possession Time .29:34	30:26	
Sacks By: Number-Yards 2-12	6-50	

RUSHING: Kansas Jayhawks-Winbush, David 14-75; Norris, Moran 11-45; Wier, Brandon 1-26; Mills, Derick 1-0; Smith, Dylen 18-minus 27. Oklahoma Sooners-Griffin, Q. 14-55; Savage, Antwone 1-40; Works, Renaldo 5-9; Littrell, Seth 1-4; Heupel, Josh 4-4; TM 3-minus 14.

PASSING: Kansas Jayhawks-Smith, Dylen 12-29-5-258. Oklahoma Sooners-Heupel, Josh 29-43-0-346.

RECEIVING: Kansas Jayhawks-Hill, Harrison 8-144; Ross, Roger 3-117; Fulton,Termaine 1-minus 3. Oklahoma Sooners-Norman, Josh 5-98; Woolfolk, Andre 5-59; Mackey, Damian 5-33; Fagan, Curtis 3-61; Griffin, Q. 3-49; Savage, Antwone 3-20; Littrell, Seth 2-17; Smith, Trent 2-9; Works, Renaldo 1-0.

INTERCEPTIONS: Kansas Jayhawks-None. Oklahoma Sooners-Thatcher, J.T. 3-9; Everage, B. 1-0; Jones, Ontei 1-0.

FUMBLES: Kansas Jayhawks-Smith, Dylen 3-2. Oklahoma Sooners-TM 2-0; Smith, Trent 1-1; Heupel, Josh 1-0; Griffin, Q. 1-1.

Stadium: Memorial Stadium. Attendance: 74,811. Kickoff time: 2 p.m.   End of Game: 5:17. Total elapsed time: 3:17. Officials: Referee: Jon Bible; Umpire: Bob Holliday; Linesman: David Alexander; Line judge: Rusty Weir; Back judge: Ron Murphy; Field judge: Greg Burks; Side judge: Butch Clark; Temperature: 82 Wind: S-20 mph Weather: Partly Cloudy

SACKS (UA-A): Kansas Jayhawks-Whitfield, D. 1-0; Jordan, Matt 1-0. Oklahoma Sooners-Cody, Dan 1-0; Calmus, Rocky 1-0; Williams, Roy 1-0; Klein, Kory 1-0; Callens, Corey 1-0; Richardson, R. 1-0.

TACKLES (UA-A): Kansas Jayhawks-Jordan, Matt 7-2; High, Kareem 4-

5; Rogers, Marcus 6-2; Nesmith, Carl 5-2; Davison, Andrew 3-4; Culp, John 3-1; Roe, Quincy 3-1; Bullock, Victor 2-2; Lomax, Dariss 3-0; Dwyer, Nate 2-1; Murphy, Chaz 1-2; Bowers, Tim 2-0; Whitfield, D. 2-0; Ross, Roger 1-0; Hayes, Marquis 1-0; Wier, Brandon 1-0; Winbush, David 1-0; Ivey, Carl 0-1; Letourneau,Jake 0-1. Oklahoma Sooners-Williams, Roy 6-7; Marshall, T. 5-3; Everage, B. 6-1; Calmus, Rocky 6-1; Thatcher, J.T. 4-2; Callens, Corey 3-2; Strait, Derrick 3-1; Richardson, R. 3-1; Thunander, Eric 3-0; Heinecke, Cory 2-1; Steffen, Roger 1-2; Cody, Dan 1-1; Klein, Kory 1-1; Fisher, Ryan 1-0; Mackey, Damian 1-0; Jones, Ontei 0-1; Thompson, M. 0-1.

GAME NOTES:

–Oklahoma's No. 14 Associated Press ranking is the highest the Sooners have been ranked since 1995 when OU entered the Texas game ranked 13th. That game ended in a 24-24 tie.

–Entering today's contest, the Sooners had not defeated Kansas since 1995 (KU won the last three contests). The last time Oklahoma went five years without beating Kansas was from 1922-1926.

–Senior free safety J.T. Thatcher's three interceptions on the day brought his interception total to five on the season. Thatcher became the seventh Sooner in history to record three interceptions in one game. The last time a Sooner recorded three interceptions in a contest was in 1992 when Darnell Walker picked off three passes against Colorado.

–Kansas quarterback Dylen Smith's 77-yard touchdown pass to Roger Ross was the longest touchdown reception given up by the Sooners since last season against Colorado when CU's Mike Moschetti hit Javon Green for an 88-yard score.

–Kansas' first-quarter 6-3 lead marked the first time OU trailed in a game this season.

–Senior quarterback Josh Heupel's first-quarter rushing touchdown was his fourth of the season and ninth of his career.

–Kansas' 13 points in the first quarter marked the most given up by the Sooners in a quarter this season.

–Junior Jeff Ferguson's 62-yard punt in the first quarter was his sixth career punt of more than 60 yards. He also booted a 66-yard punt against Rice last week.

–On offense, the Sooners started the game in a double tight end set for the first time this season.

–Senior tight end Matt Anderson recorded his first start of the season this afternoon.

–Junior Josh Norman's five pass receptions for 98 yards this afternoon marked a personal career high for both pass receptions and total receiving yards in a game. He surpassed his previous highs last season against Louisville (three receptions, 68 yards) and Notre Dame (three receptions, 29 yards).

–Sophomore running back Quentin Griffin's 13-yard touchdown run marked his fourth rushing score of the season and tied his total touchdown output of last season.

–Senior defensive back Ontei Jones' second-quarter interception was his first of the season and third of his career.

–Redshirt-freshman free safety Brandon Everage's second-quarter interception was the second of his career (he recorded one last week versus Rice).

–Sophomore wide receiver Antwone Savage's second-quarter 40-yard touchdown run was his first career rushing touchdown.

–Today's attendance (74,811) was the largest of the season and marked the ninth-straight sellout at Memorial Stadium.

–Oklahoma's five interceptions today were its most since 1993 when the Sooners picked off five passes against Texas A&M.

–Sophomore Damian Mackey's third-quarter punt return (14 yards) was the first of his career.

–Kansas junior linebacker De'Nard Whitfield returned to Memorial Stadium today. Whitfield originally signed with OU but opted to play for Fort Scott Junior College in Kansas before attending Kansas.

–With five receptions for 33 yards, Damian Mackey has caught at least one ball in 16 straight games and surpassed Eddie Hinton as OU's all-time leader in consecutive games catching at least one pass.

–Josh Heupel recorded his 11th-career 300-plus passing game by throwing for 346 yards today.

–Heupel's 346 passing yards were the most for a Sooner quarterback against Kansas since Cale Gundy threw for 324 yards against the Jayhawks in 1993.

–Heupel's 22-yard touchdown pass to sophomore wide receiver Andre Woolfolk marked the 16th straight game that Heupel has passed for at least one touchdown.

–Quentin Griffin has made at least one catch in nine straight games. Today he caught three balls for 49 yards.

–OU's edge in time of possession (30:26 to 29:34) marked the first time this season the Sooners led their opponent in the category.

Game 5

OU 63, Texas 14
63-14: Any Questions?

DALLAS, Texas, (Oct. 7, 2000) – The 10th-ranked Oklahoma Sooners took No. 11 Texas out behind the woodshed, putting a Lone Star-sized whuppin' on the Longhorns, 63-14.

"I love that week of preparation," OU quarterback Josh Heupel said. "I love when we play road games–the game was at the Cotton Bowl in Texas–because we always listen to the opposing team's music. Nothing gets you more motivated than hearing 'The Eyes of Texas' are upon you. After this game, the eyes of the nation were on the Sooners."

Oklahoma had 28 first downs and 534 yards of total offense while the Sooner defense put the clamps on the Longhorns, holding them to 10 first downs and 154 yards of total offense.

"We were confident we could play with anyone in the nation," Heupel said. "This football team would take that challenge. We were confident against Texas for the same reason we were confident every week; because we were prepared to play."

OU never relented, creating a margin so wide that, indeed, the country took notice of Oklahoma.

"We talked about when we got up on them, we were going to cut off their air supply–no second chance at life," Heupel said. "And that's exactly what we did."

The Sooner fans also were well represented.

"There's no better feeling than getting off your bus and seeing thousands of Oklahoma fans," Heupel said.

Leading up to the game, some in the media speculated that Oklahoma's burgeoning balloon was going to burst against Texas.

"I don't mean this to be disrespectful, but I've never listened to the press," Heupel said. "That really started in my senior year of high school. I'm not going to allow someone else to put me on an emotional roller coaster. I know who and what I am as football player and person. Those people in the media aren't in the locker room and they don't fully understand what goes on. Why should I read what they have to say about something I already know about? The media is a very powerful thing if you allow it to be–different individuals take it in different ways.

"All week long, the media doubted us. At our Tuesday luncheon–even without reading the paper, you can get a sense that people are predicting what will happen. Those things never matter. We knew we weren't a favorite. So there was no need to talk about it."

Still, the onslaught left quite a mark.

"Our football team never let up," Heupel said. "No one was satisfied with the score at any point in the game, because of what had happened the year before when Texas beat us 38-28. We were going to make a statement."

Coach Bob Stoops pointed out at halftime that the lead, 42-7, didn't mean the game was over.

"Don't let up," Stoops told his team in the locker room. "Finish them off."

Yet it wasn't a case of running up the score.

"It didn't get out of hand," Heupel said. "We didn't run the score up–we scored 42 points in the first half. There was no intention of running it up just to embarrass another team or coaching staff. We played our style of football for three quarters, at which time the game was in hand."

Even Heupel didn't envision 63 points, though.

"I never dream about final scores of games," Heupel said. "I dream about being successful, making big plays and winning the game."

Oklahoma was poised for a climb in the rankings.

"This is when everyone else started to see that we had a great football team," Heupel said.

A lot of Texas fans never saw the scoreboard at the end of the game.

"When you look up in the stands in the fourth quarter and see one side completely filled with Sooner fans and the Texas side almost completely empty, there was no need to look at the scoreboard," Heuepl said. "Oklahoma and its fans should remember that day forever."

The OU locker room understandably was upbeat after the game.

"It was a great feeling in the locker room after the game. That was the beginning of everyone getting a game ball," Heupel said. "There was pride in the fact that we played a great football game, as an entire team—offense, defense and special teams."

Score by quarters

Texas Longhorns. 0   7   0   7 - 14   **Record: (3-2, 1-1)**

Oklahoma Sooners . . .14   28   14   7 - 63   **Record: (5-0, 2-0)**

Scoring summary:

First quarter

11:37 OU - Woolfolk, Andre 29 yd pass from Heupel, Josh (Duncan, Tim kick), 5-57 1:16, UT 0 - OU 7

03:30 OU - Griffin, Q. 1 yd run (Duncan, Tim kick), 11-77 4:30, UT 0 - OU 14

Second quarter

14:24 OU - Griffin, Q. 2 yd run (Duncan, Tim kick), 8-43 2:07, UT 0 - OU 21

12:40 OU - Griffin, Q. 4 yd run (Duncan, Tim kick), 2-26 0:24, UT 0 - OU 28

11:30 OU - Calmus, Rocky 41 yd interception return (Duncan, Tim kick), , UT 0 - OU 35

04:43 OU - Fagan, Curtis 8 yd run (Duncan, Tim kick), 14-81 5:35, UT 0 - OU 42

03:00 UT - Mitchell,Hodges 7 yd pass from Applewhite, M. (Stockton, Kris kick), 7-80 1:43, UT 7 - OU 42

Third quarter

13:53 OU - Griffin, Q. 3 yd run (Duncan, Tim kick), 2-24 0:18, UT 7 - OU 49

01:26 OU - Griffin, Q. 8 yd run (Duncan, Tim kick), 2-17 0:43, UT 7 - OU 56

Fourth quarter

14:09 UT - Hayter, Kenny 1 yd run (Stockton, Kris kick), 5-17 2:17, UT 14 - OU 56

09:32 OU - Griffin, Q. 1 yd run (Duncan, Tim kick), 8-73 4:37, UT 14 - OU 63

	UT	OU
FIRST DOWNS	10	28
RUSHES-YARDS (NET)	17–7	56-245
PASSING YDS (NET)	161	289
Passes Att-Comp-Int	41-20-2	28-18-0
TOTAL OFF. PLAYS-YARDS	58-154	84-534
Fumble Returns-Yards.	0-0	0-0
Punt Returns-Yards	0-0	3-65
Kickoff Returns-Yards	7-174	3-51
Interception Returns-Yards	0-0	2-66
Punts (Number-Avg)	8-37.6	1-28.0
Fumbles-Lost	2-1	4-2
Penalties-Yards	7-53	13-127
Possession Time	25:52	34:08
Sacks By: Number-Yards	1-3	4-30

RUSHING: Texas Longhorns-Mitchell,Hodges 10-20; Hayter, Kenny 2-1; Applewhite, M. 1-minus 5; Simms, Chris 4-minus 23. Oklahoma Sooners-Griffin,Q. 23-87; Works, Renaldo 14-49; Heupel, Josh 7-34; Fagan, Curtis 2-30; Savage, Antwone 1-30; Littrell, Seth 8-20; Hybl, Nate 1-minus 5.

PASSING: Texas Longhorns-Simms, Chris 11-23-1-63; Applewhite, M. 9-18-1-98. Oklahoma Sooners-Heupel, Josh 17-27-0-275; Hybl, Nate 1-1-0-14.

RECEIVING: Texas Longhorns-Williams, Roy 4-16; Mitchell,Hodges 3-31; Jones, Mike 3-23; Ellis, Artie 2-14; Edwards, Brock 2-11; Flowers, M. 2-9; Healy, Brandon 1-30; Stevens, Chad 1-20; Johnson, B.J. 1-6; Hayter, Kenny 1-1. Oklahoma Sooners-Norman, Josh 3-53; Griffin, Q. 3-45; Smith, Trent 2-57; Woolfolk, Andre 2-35; Works, Renaldo 2-22; Fagan, Curtis 2-20; Savage, Antwone 2-18; Anderson, Matt 1-20; Mackey, Damian 1-19.

INTERCEPTIONS: Texas Longhorns-None. Oklahoma Sooners-Calmus, Rocky 1-41; Thatcher, J.T. 1-25.

FUMBLES: Texas Longhorns-Jones, Mike 1-0; Flowers, M. 1-1. Oklahoma Sooners-Littrell, Seth 1-1; Norman, Josh 1-0; Works, Renaldo 1-0; Hybl, Nate 1-1.

Stadium: Cotton Bowl. Attendance: 75,587. Kickoff time: 11:10 am End of Game: 2:36 p.m . Total elapsed time: 3:26. Officials: Referee: Steve Usechek; Umpire: John Davidson; Linesman: Don Kapral; Line judge: Derick Bowers; Back judge: David Ames;
Field judge: Brad Van Vark; Side judge: Phil Laurie; Temperature: 49. Wind: N, 10-15 Weather: Rainy.

SACKS (UA-A): Texas Longhorns-Thornton, Kalen 1-0. Oklahoma Sooners-Klein, Kory 0-1; Callens, Corey 0-1; Marshall, T. 1-0; Williams, Roy 1-0; Calmus, Rocky 1-0.

TACKLES (UA-A): Texas Longhorns-Rawls, Everick 6-2; Jackson, Lee 5-3; Redding, Cory 4-4; Brown, Greg 4-3; Tubbs, Marcus 3-4; Jammer, Quentin 3-3; Thornton, Kalen 4-1; Vasher, Nathan 4-1; Pearson,Dakarai 1-4; Brooks, Ahmad 4-0; Lewis, De'Andre 2-1; Babers,Roderick 2-1; Wilkins, Marcus 0-3; Hayward, Ryan 2-0; Hampton, Casey 1-1; Walker, Joe 1-0; Davis, Leonard 1-0; McKay, Miguel 1-0; McWilliams, H. 1-0; Pittman, Cole 0-1. Oklahoma Sooners-Strait, Derrick 5-5; Marshall, T. 4-3; Williams, Roy 3-4; Everage, B. 2-4; Thompson, M. 3-1; Calmus, Rocky 2-1; Lehman, Teddy 1-2; Heinecke, Cory 1-2; McCoy, Matt 0-3; Callens, Corey 0-3; Jones, Ontei 0-3; Wilkerson, J. 1-1; Thatcher, J.T. 1-1; Steffen, Roger 1-0; Littrell, Seth 0-1; Fisher, Ryan 0-1; Klein, Kory 0-1.

GAME NOTES:

–The 11:08 kickoff time was the earliest ever in the 95th meeting between Oklahoma and Texas.

–Sophomore wide receiver Andre Woolfolk's 29-yard touchdown reception early in the first quarter was his fourth of the season.

–Senior quarterback Josh Heupel's first-quarter touchdown pass marked the 17th straight game he has thrown for at least one score.

–Sophomore running back Quentin Griffin's first-quarter reception marked the 10th-straight game he has caught at least one pass.

–With six touchdowns on the day, Griffin broke the school record for most touchdowns in a single game. He surpassed Steve Owens' five-touchdown effort against Nebraska in 1968 and Jerald Moore's five touchdowns against Oklahoma State in 1994.

–Heupel's touchdown pass brought his career total to 39.

–Sophomore wide receiver Damian Mackey has caught at least one ball in 17 straight games.

–Oklahoma's 42 first-half points were the most the Sooners scored in one half this season.

–Junior linebacker Rocky Calmus' interception in the second quarter was his first of the season and second of his career. The 41-yard interception return for a touchdown marked the first score of his career.

–Sophomore split end Curtis Fagan's eight-yard touchdown run was the first rushing touchdown of his career.

–Sophomore free safety J.T. Thatcher's third-quarter interception was his sixth of the season. The OU individual record for interceptions in a season is eight.

–Heupel's 34 yards rushing marked a game career high, surpassing his previous best of 14 yards against Rice this season.

–The 11th-ranked Longhorns are the highest-ranked opponent OU has beaten since 1993 when the Sooners beat No. 5 Texas A&M, 44-14.

–Oklahoma's 63 points were its most ever against a ranked opponent.

–OU's margin of victory (49 points) was its largest ever against a ranked opponent. The previous mark was 45 against No. 13 Texas A&M last season. It also marked the largest win against Texas (previous was 45 points in 1956 in a 45-0 final).

–The Sooners held Texas to -7 yards rushing today. Texas' previous rushing low in the OU/Texas series was 17 yards in 1985.

–This is only the fourth time in history that Texas has given up 60 points or more.

–Oklahoma's 28 first downs today were its most ever against Texas, surpassing 27 first downs made in 1993.

–Oklahoma's 534 yards of total offense were the most ever against Texas. It's only the third time in the series the Sooners have surpassed the 500-yard total. The previous high was 508 in 1973.

–The Sooners outgained Texas by 380 yards in total offense (534 to 154), breaking the previous largest differential of 334 yards set by the 1956 national championship team (502 to 168).

–OU improved to 5-0 for the first time since 1993.

–Heupel has attempted 81 straight passes without an interception. He has completed 54 passes without an interception. His last interception came against Rice on Sept. 23.

–With 275 yards passing today, Heupel upped his career total to 4,980 yards, which is second on OU's all-time list. He trails Cale Gundy (6,142).

–Oklahoma's 63 points scored were the most in a game since the 1989 season opener against New Mexico State when the Sooners were victorious, 73-3.

–The Sooners held Texas to -7 seven rushing yards on the day. The last time the Sooners held an opponent to negative rushing yardage was against North Texas (-44) in 1995.

Game 6

OU 41, Kansas State 31
Number 2 Knocked Down Ladder by Sooners

MANHATTAN, Kansas, (Oct. 14, 2000) – Number 8 Oklahoma took a big bite out of the Little Apple in Manhattan, Kansas, running up 41 points on No. 2 Kansas State.

No. 1 Nebraska is up next for Oklahoma, which last week slammed No. 11 Texas.

"Everyone talked about the coaching matchups, Bill Snyder versus Bob Stoops," OU quarterback Josh Heupel said. "Even after the Texas game, everyone else outside of our locker room still doubted us. That was never more evident than before we headed to Manhattan. Everyone was questioning how we were going to play Kansas State at Kansas State. This was evident at the Tuesday luncheon when the media was coming up with a thousand reasons why we couldn't be successful in Manhattan, from being on the road, to how great their defense was, to their winning streak at home, and even their crowd."

That crowd made itself known.

"Never before have I felt such pure hatred directed toward me when we walked out of the locker room," Heupel said. "It felt as though everyone inside that stadium hated the Oklahoma Sooners. On the bus ride over, we were still a good 10 blocks from the stadium and all you could see was that K-State purple. I've never heard a stadium louder than that."

Early in the fourth quarter, Terence Newman returned a blocked punt for a touchdown. That put K-State within a touchdown, 38-31.

"After that, the stadium just exploded," Heupel said. "When we took the huddle on the sideline after that, everyone on our team looked at each other with confidence. We knew we had to go out and score points."

OU did just that, using four minutes to go 47 yards in 12 plays to set up a field goal that iced the outcome.

"With all the momentum going the other way, if we didn't pick up first downs and score, we would have put an awful lot of pressure on our defense," Heupel said.

That confidence came from the day before.

"Before we headed out to Manhattan, we had a walk through on Friday," Heupel said. "That was the loosest we've ever been. This team wasn't scared or nervous. We knew we were going to win."

With No. 1 Nebraska looming in the next game, the Sooners were reserved after the game.

"There was no locker room celebration," Heupel said. "It was sweet, no doubt about that. There is always something special about winning a big road game. And it was great to see all of our fans who were there rush the field in Manhattan."

On the plane ride home, Seth Littrell did get a Gatorade bath–unintentionally.

"I had cramped up and ended up dumping a glass of Gatorade on Seth," Heupel said with a grin.

The game was the biggest of the season to that point. While bigger games were ahead, the importance of winning at Manhattan can't be underrated.

"This was a defining moment," Heupel said. "It showed our capabilities. We showed our poise and confidence in each other even when all the momentum wasn't on our side."

Yet OU didn't get everyone's attention, despite the impressive win.

"This game didn't silence any critics," Heupel said. "But it filled our fans with great confidence. The games were getting only bigger at that point."

GAME NOTES:

–OU improved to 6-0 on the season, its best start since 1987, after defeating then second-ranked Kansas State, 41-31, in Manhattan, Kan., Saturday. The win snapped a five-game losing streak to the Wildcats.

–The win gives OU back-to-back victories against top-10 teams for the first time since beating fifth-ranked Nebraska (20-17) and No. 9 Arkansas (42-8) in 1987. The Sooners knocked off Texas, which was ranked 10th in the coaches' poll, 63-14 last Saturday

–OU's win snapped several K-State winning steaks, including: 25 straight wins at home (last loss: Nebraska, 10-5-96); 13 consecutive wins in the month of October (last loss: Nebraska 10-4-97).

–OU's defense kept the Wildcats from scoring on the game's opening drive, which marked the first time that has happened for K-State all season, as the Cats had scored on their first drive in each of their six games this season.

–The 41 points scored by the Sooners are the most registered against K-State in Manhattan since Nebraska downed the Cats 45-8 in 1990, and the 31 first-half points by OU today are the most since Nebraska's 35.

Score by quarters

Oklahoma Sooners . . .17 14   7   3 - 41   Record: (6-0, 3-0)

Kansas State Wildcats. .7   7   3 14 - 31   Record: (6-1, 2-1)

Scoring summary:

First quarter

07:43 OU - Duncan, Tim 40 yd field goal, 6 plays, 24 yards, TOP 2:42, OU 3 - KS 0

04:19 KS - Beasley, J. 15 yd run (Rheem, Jamie kick), 7 plays, 62 yards, TOP 3:24, OU 3 - KS 7

03:57 OU - Littrell, Seth 2 yd run (Duncan, Tim kick), 1 play, 2 yards, TOP 0:22, OU 10 - KS 7

00:55 OU - Fagan, Curtis 15 yd pass from Heupel, Josh (Duncan, Tim kick), 5 plays, 52 yards, TOP 1:56, OU 17 - KS 7

Second quarter

09:31 KS - Beasley, J. 2 yd run (Rheem, Jamie kick), 4 plays, 20 yards, TOP 1:41, OU 17 - KS 14

05:23 OU - Heupel, Josh 1 yd run (Duncan, Tim kick), 8 plays, 79 yards, TOP 4:08, OU 24 - KS 14

03:18 OU - Griffin, Q. 17 yd run (Duncan, Tim kick), 4 plays, 31 yards, TOP 1:41, OU 31 - KS 14

Third quarter

09:30 OU - Savage, Antwone 74 yd pass from Heupel, Josh (Duncan, Tim kick), 8 plays, 79 yards, TOP 3:34, OU 38 - KS 14

04:57 KS - Rheem, Jamie 38 yd field goal, 13 plays, 59 yards, TOP 4:33, OU 38 - KS 17

Fourth quarter

12:39 KS - Morgan, Quincy 69 yd pass from Beasley, J. (Rheem, Jamie kick), 2 plays, 72 yards, TOP 0:51, OU 38 - KS 24

10:31 KS - Newman, Terence 16 yd blocked punt return (Rheem, Jamie kick), , OU 38 - KS 31

03:27 OU - Duncan, Tim 24 yd field goal, 12 plays, 47 yards, TOP 4:10, OU 41 - KS 31

	OU	KS
FIRST DOWNS	.23	18
RUSHES-YARDS (NET)	.36-11	33-144
PASSING YDS (NET)	.374	211
Passes Att-Comp-Int	.38-29-1	36-14-2
TOTAL OFFENSE PLAYS-YARDS . . .74-385		69-355
Fumble Returns-Yards	.0-0	0-0
Punt Returns-Yards	.2-14	3-59
Kickoff Returns-Yards	.5-167	3-79
Interception Returns-Yards	.2-18	1-0
Punts (Number-Avg)	.5-35.2	7-39.6
Fumbles-Lost	.1-0	0-0
Penalties-Yards	.7-44	8-68
Possession Time	.34:29	25:31
Sacks By: Number-Yards	.0-0	4-39

RUSHING: Oklahoma Sooners-Griffin, Q. 19-23; Savage, Antwone 1-13; Norman, Josh 1-11; Littrell, Seth 4-6; TEAM 1-minus 2; Fletcher, P. 1-minus 5; Heupel, Josh 9-minus 35. Kansas State-Allen, David 9-60; Beasley, J. 15-39; Scobey, Josh 6-33; Morgan, Quincy 2-9; Cartwright, Roc 1-3.

PASSING: Oklahoma Sooners-Heupel, Josh 29-37-0-374; Works, Renaldo 0-1-1-0. Kansas State-Beasley, J. 14-36-2-211.

RECEIVING: Oklahoma Sooners-Savage, Antwone 7-116; Norman, Josh 6-93; Griffin, Q. 6-46; Fagan, Curtis 4-53; Woolfolk, Andre 3-52; Smith, Trent 3-14. Kansas State-Morgan, Quincy 5-123; Allen, David 3-25; Lockett, Aaron 3-25; Lazetich, Johnno 1-27; Wesley, Martez 1-22; Meier, Shad 1-minus 11.

INTERCEPTIONS: Oklahoma Sooners-Williams, Roy 1-18; Jones, Ontei 1-0. Kansas State-McGraw, Jon 1-0.

Stadium: KSU Stadium. Attendance: 53,011. Kickoff time: 2:30; End of Game: 6:05; Total elapsed time: 3:35; Officials: Referee: Tom Ahlers; Umpire: Jim Jankowski; Linesman: Curtis Graham; Line judge: Ron Underwood; Back judge: Mark Johnson; Field judge: Scott Gaines; Side judge: Duane Osborne; Temperature: 70. Wind: S 10-15; Weather: Mostly cloudy

SACKS (UA-A): Oklahoma Sooners-None. Kansas State-Beisel, Monty 2-0; McGraw, Jon 1-0; Fatafehi, Mario 1-0.

TACKLES (UA-A): Oklahoma Sooners-Williams, Roy 7-0; Callens, Corey 5-2; Marshall, T. 6-0; Strait, Derrick 4-1; Calmus, Rocky 4-1; Thatcher, J.T. 3-0; Jones, Ontei 2-0; Heinecke, Cory 2-0; Everage, B. 1-1; Klein, Kory 1-0; Wilson-Guest, J 1-0; Lehman, Teddy 1-0; Duncan, Tim 1-0; Woolfolk, Andre 1-0; Steffen, Roger 0-1. Kansas State-McGraw, Jon 8-1; Beisel, Monty 6-1; Butler, J. 6-1; Proctor, Milton 4-2; Fatafehi, Mario 5-0; Lott, Warren 3-2; Johnson, Chris 3-1; Cooper, Jarrod 3-1; Leber, Ben 3-0; Tyler, DeRon 3-0; Carter, Dyshod 1-2; Pierce, Terry 2-0; Newman, Terence 1-1; Libel, Brice 1-1; Holloman, Cliff 1-0; Robertson, John 1-0; Robinson, DeVane 1-0; Washington, R. 1-0; Klocke, Andy 0-1.

Game 8

OU 31, Nebraska 14
Nebraska Beef: It's What's for (OU's) Dinner

NORMAN, Oklahoma, (Oct. 28, 2000) – One game after taking down No. 2 Kansas State, No. 3 Oklahoma made a land-rush claim to the top spot after pounding No. 1 Nebraska, outscoring the Huskers 31-0 over the final three quarters of the game.

"I've never seen an atmosphere like it was," OU quarterback Josh Heupel said. "It was a three-ring circus. There was a band outside the stadium, with electric guitars and everything. ESPN's Game Day was there to win. ESPN's Lee Corso picked us, but that's just because we were at home."

Nebraska scored just 14 points–the same total Rice put up against OU–and didn't have any answers for the Sooners, going scoreless after the two first-quarter touchdowns.

"When Nebraska was up 14-0 after the first quarter, I could hear everyone in the crowd just sighing, wondering what is going on," Heupel said. "In some circles, I'd guess there were folks leaving the bandwagon. Hey, some were probably looking for the nearest bridge, because they remember what Nebraska did to Oklahoma the last few meetings–I wasn't here, but I heard it wasn't pretty."

However, OU coach Bob Stoops wasn't rattled.

"Coach Stoops never said anything when we were down," Heupel said. "Offensively, we knew that we just had to go out and execute and we'd be able to put points on the board. We completely believed in our defense–that they would play good football and adjust to shut Nebraska down. That was what was special about this football team; we had confidence in each other. When one side wasn't going well, the other side would make it up."

The tide turned in the second quarter–for good.

"The only difference between the first and second quarters, offensively, is that we settled down and began to execute," Heupel said. "There were some things we could have taken advantage of in the first quarter, but we didn't."

Two catches that didn't go for touchdowns were memorable.

"It was an offensive explosion that was capped by great plays by Andre Woolfolk and Antwone Savage–the two best catches of the season, I would say," Heupel said.

Still, the defensive effort by OU was unforgettable over the final three quarters.

"Our defense played unbelievable football," Heupel said. "I've never seen a defense play that well against that kind of option offense. Our defense was fundamentally sound filling the gaps and forcing Nebraska to get away from its base offense and do things that it doesn't have to do a lot–like throw the ball."

Score by quarters

Nebraska Cornhuskers 14   0   0   0 - 14   Record: (7-1, 4-1)

Oklahoma Sooners 0   24   7   0 - 31   Record: (7-0, 4-0)

Scoring summary:

First quarter

12:02 NU - Davison, Matt 39 yd pass from Crouch, Eric (Brown, Josh kick), 6-76 2:58, NU 7 - OU 0

08:11 NU - Crouch, Eric 37 yd run (Brown, Josh kick), 5-91 1:49, NU 14 - OU 0

Second quarter

14:13 OU - Griffin, Q. 1 yd run (Duncan, Tim kick), 9-74 2:30, NU 14 - OU 7

10:52 OU - Fagan, Curtis 34 yd pass from Heupel, Josh (Duncan, Tim kick), 5-80 2:11, NU 14 - OU 14

06:06 OU - Duncan, Tim 19 yd field goal, 4-2 1:59, NU 14 - OU 17

02:41 OU - Norman, Josh 8 yd run (Duncan, Tim kick), 4-54 1:43, NU 14 - OU 24

Third quarter

10:23 OU - Strait, Derrick 32 yd interception return (Duncan, Tim kick), NU 14 - OU 31

	NU	OU
FIRST DOWNS 16		20
RUSHES-YARDS (NET) 43-195		35-118
PASSING YDS (NET) 133		300
Passes Att-Comp-Int 27-12-1		34-20-1
TOTAL OFFENSE PLAYS-YARDS . . .70-328		69-418
Fumble Returns-Yards 0-0		0-0
Punt Returns-Yards 1-2		4-40

Kickoff Returns-Yards 3-29	2-33
Interception Returns-Yards 1-0	1-32
Punts (Number-Avg) 7-42.4	5-43.0
Fumbles-Lost 2-1	0-0
Penalties-Yards 4-50	4-21
Possession Time .31:05	28:55
Sacks By: Number-Yards 3-13	3-23

RUSHING: Nebraska Cornhuskers-Crouch, Eric 24-103, Miller, Willie 4-50, Alexander,Dan 8-25, Buckhalter,C. 5-15, Newcombe, Bobby 2-2. Oklahoma Sooners-Griffin, Q. 21-52, Heupel, Josh 8-46, Savage, Antwone 1-13, Norman, Josh 1-8, Littrell, Seth 1-1, Mackey, Damian 1-1, TM 1-minus 1, Fagan, Curtis 1-minus 2.

PASSING: Nebraska Cornhuskers-Crouch, Eric 12-27-1-133. Oklahoma Sooners-Heupel, Josh 20-34-1-300.

RECEIVING: Nebraska Cornhuskers-Newcombe, Bobby 5-26, Davison, Matt 4-79, Wistrom,Tracey 2-23, Gibson, John 1-5. Oklahoma Sooners-Fagan, Curtis 6-95, Woolfolk, Andre 5-66, Savage, Antwone 3-58, Mackey, Damian 2-16, Griffin, Q. 2-minus 2, Norman, Josh 1-45, Littrell, Seth 1-16, Works, Renaldo 0-6.

INTERCEPTIONS: Nebraska Cornhuskers-Watchorn,Troy 1-0. Oklahoma Sooners-Strait, Derrick 1-32.

FUMBLES: Nebraska Cornhuskers-Davison, Matt 1-1, Newcombe, Bobby 1-0. Oklahoma Sooners-None.

Stadium: Memorial Stadium. Attendance: 75,989. Kickoff time: 11:09 am End of Game: 2:12 p.m. Total elapsed time: 3:03. Officials: Referee: Laurie, John, Umpire: Whittenburg, R., Linesman: Crowley, Tim, Line judge: Liner, Mike, Back judge: Ryan, Rocky, Field judge: Lamberth, Jeff, Side judge: Robison, John. Temperature: 70. Wind: SE 10-15 Weather: Partly cloudy

SACKS (UA-A): Nebraska Cornhuskers-Vanden Bosch,K. 1-0, Stella,Randy 1-0, Lohr,Jason 1-0. Oklahoma Sooners-Marshall, T. 2-0, 99 1-0.

TACKLES (UA-A): Nebraska Cornhuskers-Stella,Randy 5-5, Polk, Carlos 4-5, Groce, DeJuan 6-0, Lohr,Jason 4-2, Swiney, Erwin 5-0, Craver, Keyuo 2-3, Watchorn,Troy 3-1, Walker,Joe 1-2, Vedral, Mark 1-2, Vanden Bosch,K. 1-2, Kelsay,Chris 1-1, Burrow,Jamie 1-1, Ricketts,Pat 1-1, Booker, Dion 0-2, Slechta,Jeremy 0-2, Amos, Willie 1-0, Shanle,Scott 1-0, Smith,Justin 1-0, Adams,Demoine 0-1, Penny,Jon 0-1, Clanton,Jon 0-1, Wichmann,J.P. 0-1. Oklahoma Sooners-Calmus, Rocky 6-10, Marshall, T. 8-4, Williams, Roy 4-6, Ever-age, B. 2-5, Steffen, Roger 5-1, Thompson, M. 5-1, Wilson-Guest, J 2-1, Thatcher, J.T. 2-1, Strait, Derrick 2-1, Heinecke, Cory 2-0, Jones, Ontei 2-0, Wilkerson, J. 1-1, Callens, Corey 0-2, Richardson, R. 1-0, 99 1-0, Norman, Josh 1-0, Klein, Kory 0-1.

GAME NOTES:

–This is the seventh time OU has played a No. 1-ranked team in Norman and it is the first time the Sooners have won.

–With the win today, Oklahoma upped its all-time record against No. 1-ranked teams to 6-11-2.

–The last time the Sooners beat the No. 1-ranked team in the country was in 1987 at Nebraska. OU won 17-7 on Nov. 21, 1987.

–Oklahoma is 4-0 under Head Coach Bob Stoops against teams ranked in the top 10. Last year the Sooners beat 10th-ranked Texas A&M, 51-6. This year OU has beaten 10th-ranked Texas, 63-14, second-ranked Kansas State, 41-31, and top-ranked Nebraska, 31-14.

–Nebraska's 14 points in the first quarter were the most by an opponent in the first period against a Bob Stoops-coached OU team. The last time Oklahoma gave up 14 points in the first quarter was in 1998 versus Texas.

–The 24 points by Oklahoma in the second quarter were the most points given up by Nebraska in a quarter since Colorado scored 24 last year in the fourth quarter.

–Nebraska scored touchdowns on its first two possessions but did not score the final 12 times it had the ball.

–Senior quarterback Josh Heupel passed for exactly 300 yards today, easily breaking the OU previous best against the Cornhuskers (Danny Bradley racked up 187 passing yards in 1983). In fact, Heupel threw for 238 yards in the first half today.

–Heupel's 346 yards of total offense were the most ever by an OU player versus Nebraska. Quarterback Jack Mildren held the previous school best versus the Huskers when he accounted for 267 yards in the 1971 "Game of the Century."

–Heupel's 21-yard run in the first quarter established a career long. His previous long was 16 yards against Texas this season. Heupel also set a career best in rushing yards with 46 net rushing yards. His previous best was 34 yards against Texas earlier this year.

–In the second quarter, Heupel was 7-for-10 with 149 yards and one touchdown.

–Heupel's interception in the third quarter snapped a string of 145 straight attempts and 100 consecutive completions without an interception.

–Heupel passed for at least 300 yards in a game for the 13th time in his career. He was 20-for-34 for 300 yards with one touchdown and one interception.

–Heupel has thrown a touchdown pass in each of his 19 games at Oklahoma. He connected with Curtis Fagan today for a 34-yard strike.

–Tim Duncan's 19-yard field goal gave Oklahoma a 17-14 lead with 6:06 to go in the second quarter. The boot gave the Sooners their first lead against the Cornhuskers since 1993 when OU scored to make it 7-0 with 9:44 to go in the first quarter.

–With his two catches in today's game, sophomore running back Quentin Griffin upped his season total to 22, breaking Michael Thornton's OU season record of 21 catches by a running back set last year.

–Quentin Griffin's touchdown run in the first quarter was his 12th rushing touchdown in his last four games.

–Curtis Fagan set a personal game best in receiving yards with 95, breaking his previous high of 77 yards set against Oklahoma State in 1999.

–The crowd of 75,989 was the largest in Memorial Stadium's current configuration. It was also the 10th-largest crowd in OU's home history.

–With today's victory over Nebraska, OU extended its home win streak to 12 games.

Game 8

OU 56, Baylor 7
Bears Can't Slow Top-ranked Sooners

WACO, Texas, (Nov. 4, 2000) – Perched at No. 1, Oklahoma showed no signs of slowing down.

Baylor was a blip on the radar screen, falling 56-7.

"Not much was said about us being the No. 1-ranked team in the nation," OU quarterback Josh Heupel said "Those things will go just as fast as they came if you don't take care of the important things."

The fan turnout was good–from Oklahoma's end of it.

"It was special to walk into their stadium and see so much crimson-and-cream," Heupel said. "There was no stopping our fans after the Nebraska game."

Heupel's day was short since the Sooners were up 42-0 at the half.

"Baylor was a game where we needed to go out and execute," Heupel said. "We had to focus on ourselves and everything would be all right. Our football team had an end objective. To do that, you had to be focused. We took care of business very early, making sure they had no sense of life. I don't think you would've ever known that we were the No. 1 team in the nation. Our preparation, our confidence and our focus was the same."

Score by quarters

Oklahoma Sooners . . .28   14   14   0 - 56   **Record: (8-0, 5-0)**

Baylor Bears 0   0   7   0 - 7   **Record: (2-7, 0-6)**

Scoring summary:

First quarter

11:03 OU - Thatcher, J.T. 60 yd punt return (Duncan, Tim kick), , OU 7 - BU 0

08:08 OU - Heupel, Josh 4 yd run (Duncan, Tim kick), 5 plays, 69 yards, TOP 2:23, OU 14 - BU 0

04:57 OU - Fagan, Curtis 9 yd pass from Heupel, Josh (Duncan, Tim kick), 5 plays, 25 yards, TOP 1:56, OU 21 - BU 0

01:56 OU - Fagan, Curtis 43 yd pass from Heupel, Josh (Duncan, Tim kick), 4 plays, 67 yards, TOP 1.58, OU 28 - BU 0

Second quarter

09:13 OU - Griffin, Q. 2 yd run (Duncan, Tim kick), 16 plays, 80 yards, TOP 5:34, OU 35 - BU 0

01:42 OU - Littrell, Seth 39 yd pass from Heupel, Josh (Duncan, Tim kick), 6 plays, 79 yards, TOP 2:16, OU 42 - BU 0

Third quarter

09:20 BU - James, Odell 18 yd interception return (Andino, Daniel kick), OU 42 - BU 7

08:02 OU - Fagan, Curtis 36 yd pass from Hybl, Nate (Duncan, Tim kick), 3 plays, 65 yards, TOP 1:18, OU 49 - BU 7

03:55 OU - Savage, Antwone 31 yd pass from Hybl, Nate (Duncan, Tim kick), 9 plays, 64 yards, TOP 3:06, OU 56 - BU 7

	OU	BU
FIRST DOWNS	30	7
RUSHES-YARDS (NET)	39-129	28-69
PASSING YDS (NET)	387	25
Passes Att-Comp-Int	38-25-2	30-9-2
TOTAL OFF. PLAYS-YARDS	77-516	58-94
Fumble Returns-Yards	0-0	0-0
Punt Returns-Yards	8-145	4-30
Kickoff Returns-Yards	0-0	5-98
Interception Returns-Yards	2-0	2-18
Punts (Number-Avg)	5-42.8	12-43.7
Fumbles-Lost	0-0	1-0
Penalties-Yards	7-46	6-51
Possession Time	34:32	25:28
Sacks By: Number-Yards	2-8	1-1

RUSHING: Oklahoma Sooners-Works, Renaldo 16-46; Griffin, Q. 11-40; Heupel, Josh 2-15; Hunt, Jay 1-13; Savage, Antwone 2-12; Fletcher, P. 2-6; Mackey, Damian 1-1; Hybl, Nate 2-0; Mozee, Jamar 1-0; Kuhn, Buster 1-minus 4. Baylor Bears-Bush, Darrell 11-37; Ricks, Chedrick 5-12; Golden, J. 5-10; Dixon, Kerry 6-7; Zachary, Josh 1-3.

PASSING: Oklahoma Sooners-Heupel, Josh 21-29-0-313; Hybl, Nate 4-9-2-74. Baylor Bears-Tomcheck, Guy 5-17-0-10; Dixon, Kerry 2-9-1-9; Zachary, Josh 2-4-1-6.

RECEIVING: Oklahoma Sooners-Woolfolk, Andre 7-110; Savage, Antwone 6-82; Fagan, Curtis 3-88; Littrell, Seth 2-49; Griffin, Q. 2-14; Works, Renaldo 1-25; Smith, Trent 1-14; Mackey, Damian 1-4; Donley, Lance 1-1; Norman, Josh 1-0. Baylor Bears-Newhouse, R. 3-9; Quiroga, Robert 2-6; Schoessow, C. 2-5; Fuller, Andra 1-4; Obriotti, A. 1-1.

INTERCEPTIONS: Oklahoma Sooners-Jones, Ontei 2-0. Baylor Bears-Gillenwater, R. 1-0; James, Odell 1-18.

Stadium: Floyd Casey Stadium   Attendance: 31,106. Kickoff time: 1:00 pm
End of Game: 4:06 pm   Total elapsed time: 3:06. Officials: Referee: Hal Dowden; Umpire: Richard Brown; Linesman: Al Green; Line judge: Rusty Weir; Back judge: Will Weisbrook; Field judge: Brad Horchem; Side judge: Duane Osborne; Scorer: Dave Ross; Temperature: 68. Wind: N 10. Weather: Overcast and damp

   SACKS (UA-A): Oklahoma Sooners-Richardson, R. 0-1; Wilkerson, J. 1-0; Williams, Roy 0-1. Baylor Bears-Simmons, Joe 1-0.
   TACKLES (UA-A): Oklahoma Sooners-Wilkerson, J. 6-2; Williams, Roy 3-4; Everage, B. 2-3; Jones, Ontei 4-0; Strait, Derrick 2-2; Steffen, Roger 2-2; McCoy, Matt 2-1; Richardson, R. 1-2; Calmus, Rocky 1-2; Lehman, Teddy 1-1; holleyman, B. 0-2; Mayhew, Matt 1-0; Fisher, Ryan 1-0; Thatcher, J.T. 1-0; Fletcher, P. 1-0; Littrell, Seth 1-0; Savage, Antwone 1-0; Woolfolk, Andre 1-0; Smith, Trent 0-1; Marshall, T. 0-1; Wilson-Guest, J 0-1; Callens, Corey 0-1; Cody, Dan 0-1; Panter, Ben 0-1; Ozumba, Chike 0-1; Babb, Brandon 0-1. Baylor Bears-Baxter, Gary 2-4; James, Odell 0-6; Clay, Eric 4-1; Micheaux, Kris 3-2; Amendola, Matt 2-3; Simmons, A. 2-3; Stevenson, K. 2-3; Al-Amin, Samir 4-0; Staudt, Kyle 3-1; Wilturner, D. 3-1; Phillips, D. 1-3; Hicks, Travis 0-4; Giddens, Eric 2-1; Bowie, McKinley 1-2; Hart, Bobby 1-2; Lard, Aaron 1-2; Simmons, Joe 2-0; Gillenwater, R. 1-1; Johnson, Matt 1-1; Garrett, John 1-0; Davis, Randy 1-0; Dozier, Anthony 0-1; Hall, Charles 0-1; Stiles, Adam 0-1; Williams, Kyle 0-1.

   GAME NOTES:
   –J.T. Thatcher's 60-yard punt return for a touchdown was his second of the season and third of his career. He became the first OU player to return more than one punt for a touchdown in a season since Eddie Hinton in 1966.
   –Thatcher moved into second place in the single-season punt return yards with 475 yards. He also moved into fourth place all-time in career punt return yards with 621 yards. Thatcher also ranks second in career punt return average with a 21.4 clip.
   –Andre Woolfolk's 57-yard reception in the second quarter was the longest of his career.
   –Josh Heupel's 10-yard touchdown strike to Curtis Fagan marked 20th straight game he has thrown a touchdown pass.
   –Fagan has scored a touchdown either rushing or receiving in four-straight games. In his previous 16 games he had scored only two touchdowns.

—Fagan's second touchdown catch in the first quarter marked the first multi-touchdown game of his career. He finished the day with three touchdowns.

—Fagan's three receiving touchdowns tied the school game record. The only other Sooner to catch three touchdown passes in a game was Jack Lockett in 1950 against Oklahoma State.

—Oklahoma's 28 first-quarter points were its most since scoring 28 in the second quarter against Texas on Oct. 7. OU did not score 28 points in a quarter all of last season.

—Baylor's interception return for a touchdown was the first score against the Sooners in five quarters. The OU defense has not allowed a point over seven quarters.

—With 150 yards in the first quarter, Heupel has thrown for more than 100 yards in the opening period five times this season.

—Renaldo Works' 25-yard reception was the longest of his career.

—Woolfolk's seven catches and 110 yards were both career bests.

—Seth Littrell's 39-yard touchdown catch was the longest of his career

—Heupel's 313 passing yards in the first half is an OU record. It marks the 14th time in 20 games he has thrown for more than 300 yards.

—Heupel has thrown at least two touchdown passes in 15 of his 20 games.

—Heupel became OU's all-time leader in pass attempts with 773 career attempts. He already holds career records for completions (495), touchdown passes (45), 300-yard passing games (14). He is also on the verge of breaking three other career records: passing yards (5,967, record-6,142), total offense (6,031, record-6,309) and completion percentage (.640, record-.642).

—Nate Hybl's 36-yard scoring strike to Fagan was his first career touchdown pass.

—Antwone Savage's blocked punt was OU's second in as many games. Prior to this season the last time OU had blocked a punt was in 1997 against Syracuse.

—In OU's 56-7 win, OU set series best for points scored and margin of victory.

—OU has broken the half-century mark four times in the Bob Stoops era.

—Jimmy Wilkerson recorded his first sack.

—Hybl set career highs in touchdowns (two), attempts (nine), completions (four) and yards (74).

—Ontei Jones' two interceptions mark the first multi-interception game of his career. He has intercepted four passes this season.

—Jay Hunt, Jamar Mozee and Buster Kuhn both registered their first career carry. Hunt gained 13 yards, Mozee was held to no yards and Kuhn was stopped for a four-yard loss.

–Oklahoma played four quarterbacks today.

–OU held Baylor to 94 yards total offense. The last time the Sooners held a team to less than 100 yards total offense was in 1995 when it limited North Texas to 91 yards.

Game 9

No. 1 OU 35, No. 23 Texas A&M 31

Aggies Not Enough for Oklahoma

COLLEGE STATION, Texas (Nov. 11, 2000) – Number 23 Texas A&M had a lot on the line against No. 1 Oklahoma.

Not only Big 12 ramifications, but avenging an embarrassing 51-6 defeat at the hands of the Sooners the year before in Norman.

"After the victory we had the year before against them, you knew that their coaches and team were pointing at this game all year long," Heupel said.

The game was close.

"There was no pressure being No. 1–that was never a factor," Heupel said. "The pressure we faced as a football team was that all of our goals came to pass. This was just another step."

Torrance Marshall's 41-yard interception return for a touchdown midway through the final period capped a 22-point fourth quarter for OU, and sealed the game.

"Torrance's play was maybe the biggest of the season," Heupel said. "He is one of the fiercest competitors I've ever met."

The fans in College Station were respectful but vociferous.

"No place was consistently louder throughout the game," Heupel said. "Offensively, we thought if we picked up a few first downs early, the crowd would quite down. Not only did they not quiet down, they got louder."

The Sooners never put the game out of reach.

"We struggled offensively all day long," Heupel said. "That was the first time a defense truly dropped and played a lot of zone defense against us. We didn't take full advantage of that."

A saving grace for the OU offense was its performance on clutch downs.

"Offensively we were able to make a few key plays on third downs," Heupel said.

Heupel was hearing about how he was a Heisman candidate. He thought about it none.

"I never watched or listened to any of the talk about the Heisman, except what I picked up at our Tuesday luncheons in the Switzer Center and then what I heard in the locker room after the games from the media," Heupel said. "Another important factor in us being successful as a football team is no one cared who was getting all the press attention. Because of that, our team was close and had great chemistry and truly enjoyed playing. I've never been a team that was like that before. I had been on close teams, but nothing like this. But there is something different about a championship team. There's something special you couldn't put your finger on."

GAME NOTES:

–Josh Norman's 55-yard catch in the first quarter was a career long. His previous best was a 52-yarder last year against Louisville.

–Josh Heupel's interception was his first in 54 attempts (including 38 completions).

–Heupel is now OU's all-time leader in both passing yards (6,230) and total offense (6,320).

–With 263 yards, Heupel has now thrown for at least 200 yards in 19 of 21 career games. He also extended his streak of games with a touchdown pass and games with a completion rate over 50 percent to 21 straight games.

–Antwone Savage set a career high with eight catches, giving him 44 receptions on the season. He becomes just the fifth Sooner receiver to catch 40 passes in a season and has moved into a tie for third on the all-time season-season catches. He also moved into fifth place (75) on the career receptions list.

–Savage and Quentin Griffin both extended their consecutive games with a catch streak to 14. This ties them for third best in OU history.

–Griffin rushed for two touchdowns today, marking this his third multi-touchdown game of the season.

Score by Quarters

Oklahoma 3   7   3 22 - 35   **Record: (9-0, 6-0)**

Texas A&M 7   10   7   7 - 31   **Record: (7-3, 5-2)**

Scoring Summary:

First quarter

09:14 TA - Farris, Mark 2 yd run (Kitchens, Tere. kick), 5-12 2:03, OU 0 - TA 7

07:39 OU - Duncan, Tim 31 yd field goal, 6-57 1:35, OU 3 - TA 7

Second quarter

12:48 OU - Fagan, Curtis 7 yd pass from Heupel, Josh (Duncan, Tim kick), 4-37 1:57, OU 10 - TA 7

02:53 TA - Kitchens, Tere. 37 yd field goal, 7-14 2:51, OU 10 - TA 10

00:19 TA - Ferguson,Robert 4 yd pass from Farris, Mark (Kitchens, Tere. kick), 6-39 1:49, OU 10 - TA 17

Third quarter

09:00 TA - Toombs, Ja'Mar 1 yd run (Kitchens, Tere. kick), 7-53 3:15, OU 10 - TA 24

01:46 OU - Duncan, Tim 27 yd field goal, 10-48 4:05, OU 13 - TA 24

Fourth quarter

14:46 OU - Griffin, Q. 21 yd run (Anderson, Matt pass), 3-42 0:44, OU 21 - TA 24

13:36 TA - Toombs, Ja'Mar 27 yd run (Kitchens, Tere. kick), 7-80 1:10, OU 21 - TA 31

07:43 OU - Griffin, Q. 2 yd run (Duncan, Tim kick), 15-77 5:53, OU 28 - TA 31

07:18 OU - Marshall, T. 41 yd interception return (Duncan, Tim kick), , OU 35 - TA 31

	OU	TA
FIRST DOWNS	18	18
RUSHES-YARDS (NET)	28-105	37-97
PASSING YDS (NET)	263	219
Passes Att-Comp-Int	42-28-2	37-18-2
TOTAL OFFENSE PLAYS-YARDS	70-368	74-316
Fumble Returns-Yards	0-0	1-2

Punt Returns-Yards 2-35	2-25
Kickoff Returns-Yards 3-40	3-53
Interception Returns-Yards 2-44	2-12
Punts (Number-Avg) 4-35.0	5-41.8
Fumbles-Lost 1-1	2-0
Penalties-Yards 7-74	6-60
Possession Time .29:37	30:23
Sacks By: Number-Yards 2-14	2-3

RUSHING: Oklahoma-Griffin, Q. 17-70; Heupel, Josh 8-26; Fagan, Curtis 1-13; Team 2-minus 4. Texas A&M-Toombs, Ja'Mar 18-72; Whitaker, Rich. 5-17; Goynes, Dwain 2-9; Weber, Joe 3-3; Taylor, Chris 1-2; Farris, Mark 8-minus 6.

PASSING: Oklahoma-Heupel, Josh 28-42-2-263. Texas A&M-Farris, Mark 18-37-2-219.

RECEIVING: Oklahoma-Savage, Antwone 8-76; Fagan, Curtis 6-42; Griffin, Q. 3-42; Smith, Trent 3-18; Woolfolk, Andre 3-16; Norman, Josh 2-57; Mackey, Damian 2-2; Anderson, Matt 1-10. Texas A&M-Ferguson,Robert 8-105; Porter, Greg 3-47; Johnson, Bethel 2-37; Taylor, Chris 2-16; Whitaker, Rich. 2-13; Madison, Lonnie 1-1.

INTERCEPTIONS: Oklahoma-Thompson, M. 1-3; Marshall, T. 1-41. Texas A&M-Glenn, Jason 1-12; Kiel, Terrence 1-0.

FUMBLES: Oklahoma-Woolfolk, Andre 1-1. Texas A&M-Farris, Mark 1-0; Taylor, Chris 1-0.

Stadium: Kyle Field. Attendance: 87188. Kickoff time: 12:07 PM End of Game: 3:37 PM Total elapsed time: 3:30. Officials: Referee: Randy Christal; Umpire: J.C. Leimbach; Linesman: Carl Johnson; Line judge: Kelly Deterding; Back judge: Mike Weir; Field judge: Scott Koch; Side judge: M. Weatherford; Scorer: Tom Reber; Temperature: 55. Wind: E 8. Weather: 74 % humidity

SACKS (UA-A): Oklahoma-Richardson, R. 1-0; Williams, Roy 1-0. Texas A&M-Gamble, Brian 1-0; Flemons, Ronald 1-0.

TACKLES (UA-A): Oklahoma-Calmus, Rocky 3-10; Williams, Roy 5-5; Jones, Ontei 4-4; Marshall, T. 3-4; Everage, B. 1-6; Strait, Derrick 1-6; Thompson, M. 3-2; Heinecke, Cory 2-3; Callens, Corey 2-1; Fisher, Ryan 2-1; Richardson, R. 2-1; Klein, Kory 1-1; Steffen, Roger 0-2; Romero, Frank 1-0; Savage, Antwone 1-0; holleyman, B. 0-1; Littrell, Seth 0-1. Texas A&M-Gamble, Brian 6-5; Kiel, Terrence 6-1; Bradley, Roylin 6-0; Anthony, Corne. 3-3; Jameson,Michael 4-1; Brooks, Jay 3-2; Buhl, Jonte 2-3; Edwards, Ron 2-3; Robertson, Har. 2-3; Glenn, Jason 2-2; Flemons, Ronald 2-1; Weston, Sean 2-0; Stanford, Eric 2-0; Perroni, Evan 1-1; Young, Stephen 1-1; Morris, Jared 1-1; Pinesette, Mike 1-0; Jones, Mickey 1-0; Jordan, Robert 1-0; Smith, Linnis 1-0; Scates, Cody 0-1; Pearce, Chance 0-1; Bautovich, Wes 0-1; Warren, Ty 0-1.

Game 10

No. 1 OU 27, Texas Tech 13

Red Raiders Fall to OU

NORMAN Oklahoma (Nov. 18, 2000) – The talk all week was about Oklahoma facing Texas Tech Coach Mike Leach, who had guided Oklahoma's offense the year before, putting in place a system that helped OU back to prominence.

"It was weird having to watch their offense because the teams they already played were the teams we were preparing to play," said OU quarterback Josh Heupel. "So that kind of made it tough on us because, literally, our opponents would come in to play us after seeing the same offense the week before. It allowed the teams we were preparing for, in a sense, have an extra week of preparation for the game against us."

The Coach vs. his former team angle wasn't something the OU players bought into.

"Really I never thought about it as facing someone who had coached me the previous year," Heupel said. "The teams were going head to head and that was it."

Midway though the final period, Texas Tech scored to cut the OU lead to 21-13.

"Once again there was a situation where we needed to put a drive together and get some points offensively," Heupel said.

The Sooners answered the call, going 71 yards on 12 plays to put the game away with just under two minutes left, 27-13.

"That might have been our greatest attribute as an offense–to pick up first downs and points when it was critical or necessary," Heupel said.

The game also marked Senior Day for Oklahoma, something that, while respecting the importance of acknowledging the players' commitment, didn't help build momentum.

"It was weird having my parents and sister on the field," Heupel said. "It's odd having such mental focus, and then have to step outside of that for a few minutes, and then get right back into it."

Score by Quarters

Texas Tech 0	3	0	10	- 13	**Record: (7-5,3-5)**
Oklahoma Sooners 7	7	7	6	- 27	**Record: (10-0,7-0)**

Scoring Summary:

First quarter

07:35 OU - Thatcher, J.T. 85 yd interception return (Duncan, Tim kick), , TT 0 - OU 7

Second quarter

10:11 TT - Birkholz 42 yd field goal, 4 plays, -3 yards, TOP 1:29, TT 3 - OU 7

05:38 OU - Smith, Trent 6 yd pass from Heupel, Josh (Duncan, Tim kick), 11 plays, 71 yards, TOP 4:33, TT 3 - OU 14

Third quarter

07:56 OU - Works, Renaldo 5 yd run (Duncan, Tim kick), 6 plays, 51 yards, TOP 2:02, TT 3 - OU 21

Fourth quarter

10:55 TT - Birkholz 19 yd field goal, 14 plays, 45 yards, TOP 4:30, TT 6 - OU 21

07:13 TT - Baker 15 yd pass from Kingsbury (Birkholz kick), 5 plays, 40 yards, TOP 2:31, TT 13 - OU 21

01:53 OU - Griffin, Q. 3 yd run (Duncan, Tim kick blockd), 12 plays, 71 yards, TOP 5:20, TT 13 - OU 27

	TT	OU
FIRST DOWNS	22	20
RUSHES-YARDS (NET)	23-21	25-136
PASSING YDS (NET)	309	248
Passes Att-Comp-Int	62-42-2	38-24-2
TOTAL OFFENSE PLAYS-YARDS	85-330	63-384
Fumble Returns-Yards	0-0	0-0
Punt Returns-Yards	2-11	4-69
Kickoff Returns-Yards	1-18	4-70
Interception Returns-Yards	2-48	2-85
Punts (Number-Avg)	5-43.4	4-40.0
Fumbles-Lost	1-0	4-2
Penalties-Yards	4-34	11-124
Possession Time	33:35	26:25
Sacks By: Number-Yards	0-0	3-18

RUSHING: Texas Tech-Kingsbury 11-24, Williams, S. 3-8, Munlin 1-3, Easterling 1-3, Welker 1-2, Williams, R. 5-minus 3, Team 1-minus 16. Oklahoma Sooners-Griffin, Q. 14-51, Savage, Antwone 2-34, Works, Renaldo 4-19, Woolfolk, Andre 1-11, Norman, Josh 2-8, Littrell, Seth 1-8, Heupel, Josh 1-5.

PASSING: Texas Tech-Kingsbury 41-61-2-295, Peters 1-1-0-14. Oklahoma Sooners-Heupel, Josh 24-38-2-248.

RECEIVING: Texas Tech-Williams, S. 9-59, Dorris 7-71, Welker 7-69, Baker 6-50, Francis 6-27, Williams, R. 5-3, Jones 1-16, Scovell, K. 1-14. Oklahoma Sooners-Griffin, Q. 6-32, Fagan, Curtis 4-78, Norman, Josh 3-28, Woolfolk, Andre 3-23, Anderson, Matt 2-31, Savage, Antwone 2-25, Mackey, Damian 2-17, Smith, Trent 2-14.

INTERCEPTIONS: Texas Tech-Washington 1-34, McClendon 1-14. Oklahoma Sooners-Thatcher, J.T. 1-85, Strait, Derrick 1-0.

Stadium: Memorial Stadium. Attendance: 75364. Kickoff time: 2:35 pm End of Game: 5:53. Total elapsed time: 3:18 p.m. Officials: Referee: Steve Usecheck, Umpire: John Davidson, Linesman: Don Kapral, Line judge: Derick Bowers, Back judge: Randy Mcanally, Field judge: Brad Van Vark, Side judge: Phil Laurie, Temperature: 46; Wind: Variable Weather: Partly Cloudy

SACKS (UA-A): Texas Tech-None. Oklahoma Sooners-Marshall, T. 1-0, Callens, Corey 1-0, Richardson, R. 1-0.

TACKLES (UA-A): Texas Tech-Norman, John 7-2, Hunt 4-3, Pitts 3-3, Curtis 3-2, Lemons 3-2, Washington 2-3, Kocurek 1-4, Alexander 3-1, Flugence 1-3, McClendon 2-1, McCoy 1-2, Briggs 1-2, Norman, Joe 1-1, Turner 1-0, Aycock 1-0, Shain 1-0, Rasberry 0-1, Watson 0-1. Oklahoma Sooners-Calmus, Rocky 5-7, Williams, Roy 8-3, Marshall, T. 7-2, Thompson, M. 7-2, Thatcher, J.T. 5-4, Strait, Derrick 5-2, Jones, Ontei 5-1, Richardson, R. 3-2, Heinecke, Cory 3-2, Callens, Corey 2-2, Everage, B. 2-1, Chretien, M. 1-2, Littrell, Seth 2-0, Fisher, Ryan 1-1, Woolfolk, Andre 0-2, holleyman, B. 1-0, Klein, Kory 1-0, Works, Renaldo 1-0, Panter, Ben 0-1, Jackson, Brent 0-1.

GAME NOTES:

–A sellout crowd of 75,364 marked the 12th-straight sellout at Owen Field.

–Senior fullback Seth Littrell wore number 42, as a tribute to his father, former Sooner fullback Jim Littrell, who played from 1973-75, and was a part of two national championships.

–J.T. Thatcher's seventh interception of the year which he returned 85 yards for a touchdown was the eight-longest defensive score in Sooner history and the longest since Ricky Dickson's 95-yard interception return against Oklahoma State in 1987.

–Thatcher's return made him the fifth different Sooner to return an interception for a touchdown this season, he joins Roy Williams, Rocky Calmus, Derrick Strait and Torrance Marshall.

–Antwone Savage's 32-yard run on the opening play of the game brought his season total to 140 yards which is the second most in a season for a non-backfield member, the record is held by Keith Jackson, who had 153 yards in 1985.

–J.T. Thatcher's 11-yard punt return in the first quarter broke Jack Mitchell's 52-year old school record for return yards in a year.

–Antwone Savages 25 yards against Texas Tech made him the 10th Sooner in history to post over a 1,000 recieving yards in his career. Savage's career total now stands at 1,018.

–Josh Heupel's six-yard touchdown in the second quarter marked the 22nd-straight game in his career that he has thrown a touchdown pass.

–Josh Heupel's 253 total offensive yards broke Cale Gundy's career mark of 6,389 yards, which had stood since 1993. Heupel's career total now stands at 6,498.

–Today's start marked the 22nd-straight of Josh Heupel's career, he is fifth all-time on the OU career list for quarterbacks. Heupel trails only Jack Mildren (34), Steve Davis (34), Boby Womack (25) and J.C. Watts (24).

–With the win tonight, the Sooners' record improves to 42-0 versus unranked opponents while ranked No. 1.

–The win also increases Oklahoma's home record to 28-0 while ranked No. 1.

–With OU's victory over Texas Tech, the Sooners' home win streak improves to 13 straight, longest in the Big 12.

–Kicker Tim Duncan's missed point after touchdown following OU's fourth quarter touchdown was his first miss after connecting on 55-straight this season. The streak is the third longest by a Sooner in a single-season. Tim Lashar, in 1986, had 60-straight PAT's in that season and Uwe Von Schamanm had a stretch of 59-consecutive PAT's in 1978.

–J.T. Thatcher had a spectacular return against Texas Tech in the return game, returning 4 punts for 69 yards, three kickoffs for 52 yards, and 1 interception return of 85 yards for a total of 206 yards in the return game.

Game 11

No. 1 OU 12, Oklahoma State 7

OU Nudges Cowboys

STILLWATER, Oklahoma (Nov. 25, 2000) – A rival game for the No. 1 team.

And Oklahoma State, trying to send off outgoing coach Bob Simmons in style, gave the No. 1 Sooners all they could handle.

"There was nothing to be lost in that game for them," said OU quarterback Josh Heupel.

OU had 18 first downs and 309 yards of total offense, compared to 13 and 275 yards of total offense for Oklahoma State

"We did not play a very good football game," Heupel said. "In fact, offensively, we played poorly. On the first series of the game,

OSU did a good job of mixing up zone coverages with man cover-age, and blitzes. After that, they started dropping almost everyone except the defensive tackle, leaving them with two-man and three-man rushes most of the time."

The Sooners weren't looking ahead to the Big 12 Championship game.

"We just didn't play well, so credit our defense for bailing us out," Heupel said. "Our concern wasn't about the Big 12 Championship, it was about that football game against OSU."

One reason for that concern was that this game was OSU's bowl or championship game.

"This was their bowl game–their last game for this season," Heupel said. "They played extremely hard. It's a tribute to their players for playing that hard."

Score by Quarters
Oklahoma Sooners 7   5   0   0 - 12   **Record: (3-8,1-7)**
Oklahoma State 0   0   7   0 - 7   **Record: (11-0,8-0)**

Scoring Summary:
First quarter
06:35 OU - Fagan, Curtis 3 yd pass from Heupel, Josh (Duncan, Tim kick), 11 plays, 99 yards, TOP 3:51, OU 7 - OS 0
Second quarter
10:06 OU - Duncan, Tim 39 yd field goal, 5 plays, 11 yards, TOP 1:23, OU 10 - OS 0
03:10 OU - Team safety , OU 12 - OS 0
Third quarter
05:41 OS - Bell, Tatum 60 yd run (Condley, Seth kick), 1 play, 60 yards, TOP 0:11, OU 12 - OS 7

	OU	**OS**
FIRST DOWNS 18		13
RUSHES-YARDS (NET) 34-155		38-173
PASSING YDS (NET) 154		102

Passes Att-Comp-Int 36-19-2	20-9-2
TOTAL OFFENSE PLAYS-YARDS . . .70-309	58-275
Fumble Returns-Yards 0-0	0-0
Punt Returns-Yards 1-12	4-51
Kickoff Returns-Yards 2-49	1-8
Interception Returns-Yards 2-59	2-39
Punts (Number-Avg). 6-44.7	5-39.0
Fumbles-Lost 1-0	1-0
Penalties-Yards 6-50	5-35
Possession Time .29:33	30:27
Sacks By: Number-Yards 0-0	1-9

RUSHING: Oklahoma Sooners-Griffin, Q. 21-115; Heupel, Josh 7-17; Savage, Antwone 2-13; Fagan, Curtis 1-10; Littrell, Seth 1-5; Team 1-0; Norman, Josh 1-minus 5. Oklahoma State-Bell, Tatum 8-90; White, Reggie 14-44; Pogi, Aso 11-42; Burrough, Tim 2-1; Team 1-0; Fobbs, Jamaal 1-minus 2; Lindsay, Gabe 1-minus 2.

PASSING: Oklahoma Sooners-Heupel, Josh 19-36-2-154. Oklahoma State-Pogi, Aso 9-20-2-102.

RECEIVING: Oklahoma Sooners-Fagan, Curtis 6-44; Griffin, Q. 5-59; Mackey, Damian 4-36; Norman, Josh 2-11; Littrell, Seth 1-2; Savage, Antwone 1-2. Oklahoma State-Woods, Rashaun 2-26; Fobbs, Jamaal 2-22; White, Reggie 2-5; Lindsay, Gabe 1-21; Young, Willie 1-19; Jackson, Khary 1-9.

INTERCEPTIONS: Oklahoma Sooners-Thatcher, J.T. 1-35; Marshall, T. 1-24. Oklahoma State-Craig, Elbert 1-29; Carter, Chris 1-10.

Stadium: Lewis Field. Attendance: 48500. Kickoff time: 2:33   End of Game: 5:41 p.m. Total elapsed time: 3:08. Officials: Referee: Tom Ahlers; Umpire: Jim Jankowski; Linesman: Curtis Graham; Line judge: Ron Underwood; Back judge: Len Williams; Field judge: Scott Gaines; Side judge: Butch Clark; Scorer: Lee Manzer; Temperature: 53   Wind: NNW 15   Weather: Sunny, gusts to 20

SACKS (UA-A): Oklahoma Sooners-None. Oklahoma State-Thomas, Juqua 1-0.

TACKLES (UA-A): Oklahoma Sooners-Marshall, T. 6-3; Calmus, Rocky

5-4; Heinecke, Cory 5-2; Thatcher, J.T. 4-2; Williams, Roy 4-1; Thompson, M. 3-2; Strait, Derrick 4-0; Jones, Ontei 3-0; Fisher, Ryan 1-2; Steffen, Roger 1-0; Everage, B. 1-0; Wilkerson, J. 1-0; Callens, Corey 1-0; Richardson, R. 1-0; Holleyman, Bary 0-1; Griffin, Q. 0-1; Anderson, Matt 0-1; McCoy, Matt 0-1. Oklahoma State-Levels, Dwayne 6-3; Robinson, T. 6-2; Thomas, Juqua 5-3; Craig, Elbert 4-2; Carter, Chris 3-2; Gillem, Robbie 2-2; Barry, Sean 2-1; Williams, Kevin 2-1; Warner, Zac 2-1; Massey, Chris 2-0; Carter, Fath' 1-1; Jones, Paul 1-1; Cooper, Michael 1-1; Lindsay, Gabe 1-0; Jones, Marcus 1-0; Brown, LaWaylon 1-0; Riffe, Jake 1-0; Holmes, Ricklan 1-0; Davis-Bryant 1-0; Tyler, Chris 0-1; Akin, Zac 0-1.

Game 12

No. 1 OU 27, No. 8 Kansas State 24

Sooners Snare Big 12 Crown

KANSAS CITY, Missouri (Dec. 2, 2000) – Number 8 Kansas State wanted revenge, and was hoping to get back into the national championship picture.

Oklahoma was buying none of that. The top-ranked Sooners rallied for 10 fourth-quarter points to claim the Big 12 Championship and lock in a spot in the Orange Bowl for the National Championship.

The talk in the media all week was about how hard it is to beat a team twice in the same season, something OU would have to do if it was to earn its shot at a berth in the national championship game.

OU quarterback Josh Heupel said the media never mentioned that it would be hard for the losing team to play a team it had already lost to.

"I truly don't believe one team is at an advantage if you've played before during that season," Heupel said. "It was hard to beat Kansas State twice because they were a great football team, not because we had played them twice. They had a little bit of extra advantage with an extra week to play for us–they were off while we played Oklahoma State."

Still, it was a championship atmosphere in Kansas City, located on the border with Kansas, giving K-State somewhat a home-game feel despite the so-called neutral site.

"That makes it hard for a championship game, but it was a great setting," Heupel said. "There were a lot of K-State fans and a lot of Oklahoma fans. It was a great setting for college football."

OU players proved many in the media wrong, those who thought OU couldn't beat K-State twice.

"Every game throughout the season people were pinpointing reasons why we shouldn't win," Heupel said. "We were only concerned with proving them wrong. If you can't get yourself up to play for a championship game you don't deserve to put on the pads. There's an excitement about just being there and being able to play in that setting. It was a championship atmosphere.

K-State was one of the best teams OU played all year.

"We respected Kansas State but never feared them," Heupel said.

The game was tied at 10 at halftime and then at 17 to end the third quarter. OU pulled ahead by 10 with a touchdown and field goal in the fourth quarter. K-State's final points came with six seconds left in the game.

K-State coach Bill Snyder handled his second 2000 defeat at the hands of OU with class.

"I hope Oklahoma wins the national championship," Snyder said, "For the Big 12. We just weren't good enough to make a difference in the game tonight."

GAME NOTES:

–Oklahoma has now won 37 conference championships in football.

–The Sooners have qualified for the FedEx Orange Bowl. OU has appeared in 16 Orange Bowls, winning 12 of them.

–Quarterback Josh Heupel set a Big 12 record for career completions with 590, breaking the previous record held by Major Applewhite of Texas, 582.

–Heupel has now thrown for over 200 yards in 21 of his 24 games.

–Oklahoma's winning streak of 12 games is the longest current streak in the nation. They have also won 10 straight conference games.

–Bob Stoops improves to 19-5 as a head coach and his .792 winning percentage is tied with Vernon Parrington for the third-best winning percentage in Oklahoma history. Stoops is 5-0 against top 10 teams.

–The OU defense hasn't allowed an opponent over 200 yards rushing in 18 straight games.

–Josh Norman blocked his second punt of the season.

–Strong safety Roy Williams made his first career fumble recovery.

–Flanker Quentin Griffin's 29-yard run in the fourth quarter was the third long rushing play in Big 12 championship history (Priest Holmes of Texas, 61 yards in 1996 vs. Nebraska; Nebraska's Correll Buckhalter, 55 yards vs. Texas in 1999).

–Griffin now has at least one catch in 17 straight games, tying an OU record.

–Tim Duncan's nine points gives him 98 for his career, establishing a new Oklahoma record formerly held by Tim Lasher, 96 points.

Big 12 Championship Game

Score by Quarters

Kansas State 0   10   7   7 - 24   **Record: (10-3-0,6-3)**

Oklahoma 3   7   7 10 - 27   **Record: (12-0-0,9-0)**

Scoring Summary:

First quarter

07:16 OU - Duncan, Tim 33 yd field goal, 7 plays, 23 yards, TOP 1:56 0 – 3

Second quarter

14:54 KS - Beasley, J. 10 yd run (Rheem, Jamie kick) 2 plays, 11 yards, TOP 0:29 7 - 3

07:58 KS - Rheem, Jamie 22 yd field goal; 12 plays, 57 yards, TOP 5:48 10 - 3

02:56 OU - Smith, Trent 1 yd pass from Heupel, Josh (Duncan, Tim kick) 3 plays, 17 yards, TOP 1:06 10 - 10

Third quarter

05:54 OU - Heupel, Josh 7 yd run (Duncan, Tim kick) 8 plays, 69 yards, TOP 3:33 10 - 17

03:29 KS - Lockett, Aaron 58 yd punt return (Rheem, Jamie kick) 17 - 17

Fourth quarter

14:24 OU - Woolfolk, Andre 17 yd pass from Heupel, Josh (Duncan, Tim kick) 9 plays, 79 yards, TOP 4:05 17 - 24

01:25 OU - Duncan, Tim 46 yd field goal 9 plays, 54 yards, TOP 2:39 17 - 27

00:06 KS - Morgan, Quincy 16 yd pass from Beasley, J. (Rheem, Jamie kick) 6 plays, 60 yards, TOP 1:19 24 - 27

	KS	OU
FIRST DOWNS	14	15
RUSHES-YARDS (NET)	38-133	28-99
PASSING YDS (NET)	106	220
Passes Att-Comp-Int	28-12-0	44-24-3
TOTAL OFFENSE PLAYS-YARDS	66-239	72-319
Fumble Returns-Yards	0-0	0-0
Punt Returns-Yards	3-75	3-14
Kickoff Returns-Yards	6-131	1-21
Interception Returns-Yards	3-9	0-0
Punts (Number-Avg)	9-28.4	6-38.2
Fumbles-Lost	2-1	0-0
Penalties-Yards	5-42	4-30
Possession Time	30:50	29:10
Sacks By: Number-Yards	2-20	1-8

RUSHING: Kansas State-Cartwright, Rod 9-49; Beasley, J. 11-40; Scobey, Josh 9-22; Allen, David 5-22; Morgan, Quincy 1-2; Lockett, Aaron 1-1; Meier, Shad 1-1; TEAM 1-minus 4. Oklahoma-Griffin,Quentin 13-87; Heupel, Josh 11-9; Savage, Antwone 2-5; Littrell, Seth 1-0; TEAM 1-minus 2.

PASSING: Kansas State-Beasley, J. 12-28-0-106. Oklahoma-Heupel, Josh 24-44-3-220.

RECEIVING: Kansas State-Morgan, Quincy 6-57; Cartwright, Rod 2-2; Wesley, Martez 1-26; Lockett, Aaron 1-11; Allen, David 1-5; Hoheisel, Nick 1-5. Oklahoma-Smith, Trent 8-96; Griffin,Quentin 7-38; Woolfolk, Andre 2-40;

Mackey, Damian 2-21; Fagan, Curtis 2-4; Norman, Josh 1-9; Littrell, Seth 1-8; Savage, Antwone 1-4.

INTERCEPTIONS: Kansas State-Butler, J. 1-8; Carter, Dyshod 1-0; Robinson, DeVane 1-1. Oklahoma-None.

Stadium: Arrowhead Stadium. Attendance: 79655. Kickoff time: 7:08   End of Game: 10:47. Total elapsed time: 3:29. Officials: Referee: Randy Christal; Umpire: R. Whittenburg; Linesman: Carl Johnson; Line judge: Mike Liner; Back judge: John Robison; Field judge: Jeff Lamberth; Side judge: Scott Koch; Temperature: 37; Wind: ENE 3; Weather: Clear

SACKS (UA-A): Kansas State-Beisel, Monty 0-1; Togiai, Jerry 0-1; Leber, Ben 1-0. Oklahoma-Jones, Ontei 1-0.

TACKLES (UA-A): Kansas State-Cooper, Jarrod 6-3; Beisel, Monty 5-4; Fatafehi, Mario 5-2; Togiai, Jerry 2-4; Leber, Ben 4-1; Butler, J. 3-2; McGraw, Jon 1-4; Tyler, DeRon 2-2; Carter, Dyshod 1-2; Johnson, Chris 1-2; Robinson, DeVane 1-2; Kazar, Jason 0-3; Proctor, Milton 2-0; Gosch, Neil 1-0; Buhl, Josh 1-0; Pierce, Terry 0-1; Newman, Terence 0-1; Yates, Derrick 0-1. Oklahoma-Calmus, Rocky 2-7; Williams, Roy 6-2; Marshall, T. 5-2; Thatcher, J.T. 4-3; Heinecke, Corey 3-1; Woolfolk, Andre 3-1; Fisher, Ryan 3-1; Thompson, M. 2-2; Klein, Kory 2-1; Jones, Ontei 2-0; Wilkerson, Jimmy 1-1; Callens, Corey 1-1; Steffen, Roger 0-2; Strait, Derrick 0-2; Holleyman, Bary 0-2; Savage, Antwone 1-0; Skinner, Mike 1-0; Littrell, Seth 1-0; Everage,Brandon 0-1; Duncan, Tim 0-1.

Play-by-Play Summary (1st quarter)

OU won the toss, deferred. OU kicks off, defends the east goal

K 1-10 K35   OU ball on OU35.

Duncan, Tim kickoff 58 yards to the KS7, Newman, Terence return 17 yards to the KS24, PENALTY KS holding 10 yards to the KS14, 1st and 10, KS ball on KS14.

K 1-10 K14   Scobey, Josh rush for 3 yards to the KS17 (Fisher, Ryan).

K 2-7 K17   Cartwright, Rod rush for 8 yards to the KS25, 1ST DOWN KS (Heinecke, Corey).

K 1-10 K25   Beasley, J. pass incomplete to Lockett, Aaron.

K 2-10 K25   Beasley, J. rush to the KS27, fumble forced by Marshall, T., fumble by

Beasley, J. recovered by OU Williams, Roy at KS27.

————— 4 plays, 3 yards, TOP 01:41 —————

O 1-10 K27   OKLAHOMA drive start at 13:19 (1st).

O 1-10 K27   Heupel, Josh pass complete to Woolfolk, Andre for 23 yards to the KS4, 1ST DOWN OU (Carter, Dyshod).

O 1-G K04   Griffin,Quentin rush for 2 yards to the KS2 (Fatafehi, Mario;Yates, Derrick).

O 2-G K02   PENALTY OU false start 5 yards to the KS7.

O 2-G K07   Heupel, Josh pass complete to Smith, Trent for 6 yards to the KS1 (Butler, J.).

O 3-G K01   Heupel, Josh rush for no gain to the KS1 (Beisel, Monty).

O 4-G K01   Griffin,Quentin rush for loss of 1 yard to the KS2 (Fatafehi, Mario).

————— 5 plays, 25 yards, TOP 02:30 —————

K 1-10 K02   KANSAS STATE drive start at 10:49 (1st).

K 1-10 K02   Scobey, Josh rush for 1 yard to the KS3 (Williams, Roy).

K 2-9   K03   Beasley, J. pass complete to Morgan, Quincy for 2 yards to the KS5.

K 3-7   K05   Beasley, J. pass incomplete (Marshall, T.).

K 4-7   K05   Brown, Travis punt 33 yards to the KS38, fair catch by Thatcher, J.T..

————— 3 plays, 3 yards, TOP 01:37 —————

O 1-10 K38   OKLAHOMA drive start at 09:12 (1st).

O 1-10 K38   Heupel, Josh pass incomplete to Woolfolk, Andre.

O 2-10 K38   Heupel, Josh pass incomplete to Woolfolk, Andre (Carter, Dyshod).

O 3-10 K38   Heupel, Josh pass complete to Mackey, Damian for 14 yards to the KS24, 1ST DOWN OU (Carter, Dyshod;Tyler, DeRon).

O 1-10 K24   Heupel, Josh pass incomplete to Woolfolk, Andre.

O 2-10 K24   Heupel, Josh pass complete to Norman, Josh for 9 yards to the KS15 (Beisel, Monty).

O 3-1   K15   Griffin,Quentin rush for no gain to the KS15 (Leber, Ben;Beisel, Monty).

O 4-1 K15   Duncan, Tim field goal attempt from 33 GOOD, clock 07:16.

KANSAS STATE 0, OKLAHOMA 3

————— 7 plays, 23 yards, TOP 01:56 —————

Duncan, Tim kickoff 65 yards to the KS0, Lockett, Aaron return 25 yards to the KS25 (Savage, Antwone).

K 1-10 K25   KANSAS STATE drive start at 07:16 (1st).

K 1-10 K25   Scobey, Josh rush for 2 yards to the KS27 (Williams, Roy).

K 2-8   K27   Cartwright, Rod rush to the KS36, fumble forced by Heinecke, Corey, fumble by Cartwright, Rod recovered by KS Cartwright, Rod at KS36, 1ST DOWN KS.

K 1-10 K36   Beasley, J. pass complete to Morgan, Quincy for 8 yards to the KS44 (Thompson, M.).

K 2-2 K44   Allen, David rush for 6 yards to the 50 yardline, 1ST DOWN KS (Fisher, Ryan).

K 1-10 K50   Beasley, J. pass incomplete to Morgan, Quincy (Thompson, M.).

K 2-10 K50   Beasley, J. pass incomplete to Lockett, Aaron.

K 3-10 K50   Beasley, J. pass incomplete to Lockett, Aaron.

K 4-10 K50   Brown, Travis punt 36 yards to the OU14, downed.

————— 7 plays, 25 yards, TOP 02:58 —————

O 1-10 O14   OKLAHOMA drive start at 04:18 (1st).

O 1-10 O14   Griffin,Quentin rush for loss of 2 yards to the OU12 (Johnson, Chris; Robinson, DeVane).

O 2-12 O12   Heupel, Josh pass intercepted by Carter, Dyshod at the OU43, Carter,

Dyshod return 0 yards to the OU43 (Woolfolk, Andre).

————— 2 plays, minus 2 yards, TOP 00:49 —————

K 1-10 O43   KANSAS STATE drive start at 03:29 (1st).

K 1-10 O43   Scobey, Josh rush for 2 yards to the OU41 (Calmus, Rocky;Thompson, M.).

K 2-8 O41   Cartwright, Rod rush for 5 yards to the OU36 (Thatcher, J.T.;Calmus, Rocky).

K 3-3 O36   Lockett, Aaron rush for 1 yard to the OU35 (Marshall, T.).

K 4-2 O35   Beasley, J. punt 32 yards to the OU3, downed.

————— 3 plays, 8 yards, TOP 02:19 —————

O 1-10 O03   OKLAHOMA drive start at 01:10 (1st).

O 1-10 O03   Heupel, Josh pass complete to Griffin,Quentin for 6 yards to the OU9 (Butler, J.;Pierce, Terry).

O 2-4 O09   Heupel, Josh pass intercepted by Robinson,DeVane at the OU12,

Robinson,DeVane return 1 yards to the OU11 (Skinner, Mike).

————— 2 plays, 6 yards, TOP 00:47 —————

K 1-10 O11   KANSAS STATE drive start at 00:23 (1st).

K 1-10 O11   Meier, Shad rush for 1 yard to the OU10 (Calmus, Rocky).

====END OF 1st QUARTER====
KANSAS STATE 0, OKLAHOMA 3

Play-by-Play Summary (2nd quarter)

K 2-9 O10   Start of 2nd quarter, clock 15:00.

K 2-9 O10   Beasley, J. rush for 10 yards to the OU0, 1ST DOWN KS, TOUCHDOWN, clock 14:54.

Rheem, Jamie kick attempt good, PENALTY OU personal foul 15 yards to the 50 yardline.

KANSAS STATE 7, OKLAHOMA 3

————— 2 plays, 11 yards, TOP 00:29 —————

Rheem, Jamie kickoff 50 yards to the OU0, touchback.

O 1-10 O20   OKLAHOMA drive start at 14:54 (2nd), 1st and 10.

O 1-10 O20   Savage, Antwone rush for 1 yard to the OU21 (Beisel, Monty;Robinson,DeVane).

O 2-9 O21   Heupel, Josh pass incomplete to Woolfolk, Andre.

O 3-9 O21   Heupel, Josh pass incomplete to Griffin,Quentin.

O 4-9 O21   Ferguson, Jeff punt 41 yards to the KS38, out-of-bounds.

————— 3 plays, 1 yards, TOP 01:08 —————

K 1-10 K38   KANSAS STATE drive start at 13:46 (2nd).

K 1-10 K38   Cartwright, Rod rush for 7 yards to the KS45 (Strait, Derrick;Steffen, Roger).

K 2-3 K45   Cartwright, Rod rush for 2 yards to the KS47 (Marshall, T.;Fisher, Ryan).

K 3-1 K47   Scobey, Josh rush for 1 yard to the KS48, 1ST DOWN KS (Steffen, Roger;Thompson, M.).

K 1-10 K48   Beasley, J. pass complete to Morgan, Quincy for 8 yards to the OU44, out-of-bounds (Thompson, M.).

K 2-2 O44   Allen, David rush for 2 yards to the OU42, 1ST DOWN KS (Williams, Roy).

K 1-10 O42   Beasley, J. pass complete to Hoheisel, Nick for 5 yards to the OU37.

K 2-5 O37   Allen, David rush for 9 yards to the OU28, 1ST DOWN KS (Thatcher, J.T.).

K 1-10 O28   Cartwright, Rod rush for 15 yards to the OU13, 1ST DOWN KS (Heinecke, Corey).

K 1-10 O13   Timeout Kansas State, clock 10:08.

K 1-10 O13   Allen, David rush for no gain to the OU13 (Thatcher, J.T.;Calmus, Rocky).

K 2-10 O13   Allen, David rush for 5 yards to the OU8 (Marshall, T.).

K 3-5 O08   Beasley, J. rush for 3 yards to the OU5 (Klein, Kory;Calmus, Rocky).

K 4-2 O05   Rheem, Jamie field goal attempt from 22 GOOD, clock 07:58.

KANSAS STATE 10, OKLAHOMA 3

————— 12 plays, 57 yards, TOP 05:48 —————

Rheem, Jamie kickoff 65 yards to the OU0, touchback.

O 1-10 O20   OKLAHOMA drive start at 07:58 (2nd).

O 1-10 O20   Heupel, Josh pass complete to Littrell, Seth for 8 yards to the OU28, out-of-bounds (Kazar, Jason;Carter, Dyshod).

O 2-2 O28   Griffin,Quentin rush for 3 yards to the OU31, 1ST DOWN OU (Fatafehi, Mario).

O 1-10 O31   Heupel, Josh pass complete to Griffin,Quentin for 8 yards to the OU39 (Proctor, Milton).

O 2-2 O39   Griffin,Quentin rush for 1 yard to the OU40 (Togiai, Jerry).

O 3-1 O40   Heupel, Josh sacked for loss of 10 yards to the OU30 (Togiai, Jerry; Beisel, Monty).

O 4-11 O30   Ferguson, Jeff punt 44 yards to the KS26, downed.

————— 5 plays, 10 yards, TOP 02:43 —————

K 1-10 K26   KANSAS STATE drive start at 05:15 (2nd).

K 1-10 K26   PENALTY KS false start 5 yards to the KS21.

K 1-15 K21   Beasley, J. pass incomplete to Morgan, Quincy (Thompson, M.).

K 2-15 K21   Cartwright, Rod rush for 2 yards to the KS23 (Calmus, Rocky;Williams, Roy).

K 3-13 K23   Beasley, J. pass incomplete to Wesley, Martez.

K 4-13 K23   TEAM punt BLOCKED, recovered by OU Jones, Ontei at KS17, Jones, Ontei for no gain to the KS17 (Gosch, Neil) (blocked by Norman, Josh).

————— 3 plays, minus 3 yards, TOP 01:13 —————

O 1-10 K17   OKLAHOMA drive start at 04:02 (2nd), OU ball on KS17.

O 1-10 K17   Heupel, Josh pass complete to Mackey, Damian for 7 yards to the KS10 (Tyler, DeRon).

O 2-3 K10   Heupel, Josh pass complete to Griffin,Quentin for 9 yards to the KS1, 1ST DOWN OU, out-of-bounds (Butler, J.).

O 1-G K01   Heupel, Josh pass complete to Smith, Trent for 1 yard to the KS0,

TOUCHDOWN, clock 02:56.

Duncan, Tim kick attempt good.

KANSAS STATE 10, OKLAHOMA 10

————— 3 plays, 17 yards, TOP 01:06 —————

Duncan, Tim kickoff 64 yards to the KS1, Lockett, Aaron return 28 yards to the KS29 (Wilkerson,Jimmy).

K 1-10 K29   KANSAS STATE drive start at 02:56 (2nd).

K 1-10 K29   Scobey, Josh rush for loss of 2 yards to the KS27 (Thatcher, J.T.).

K 2-12 K27   Beasley, J. pass incomplete to Morgan, Quincy (Thompson, M.).

K 3-12 K27   Beasley, J. pass complete to Allen, David for 5 yards to the KS32 (Williams, Roy;Marshall, T.).

K 4-7 K32   Timeout Oklahoma, clock 01:48.

K 4-7 K32   TEAM rush for loss of 4 yards to the KS28.

————— 4 plays, minus 1 yards, TOP 01:23 —————

O 1-10 K28   OKLAHOMA drive start at 01:33 (2nd).

O 1-10 K28   Heupel, Josh pass incomplete.

O 2-10 K28   Heupel, Josh pass incomplete to Griffin,Quentin.

O 3-10 K28   PENALTY OU delay of game 5 yards to the KS33.

O 3-15 K33   Heupel, Josh pass incomplete to Littrell, Seth (Proctor, Milton).

O 4-15 K33   Duncan, Tim punt 32 yards to the KS1, downed.

————— 3 plays, minus 5 yards, TOP 00:27 —————

K 1-10 K01   KANSAS STATE drive start at 01:06 (2nd).

K 1-10 K01   Timeout Oklahoma, clock 01:06.

K 1 10 K01   Beasley, J. rush for 2 yards to the KS3 (Callens, Corey).

K 2-8 K03   Beasley, J. rush for no gain to the KS3 (Fisher, Ryan).

K 3-8 K03   End of 1st half, clock 00:00.

=====END OF 2nd QUARTER=====
KANSAS STATE 10, OKLAHOMA 10

Play-by-Play Summary (3rd quarter)

K 3-8 K03   Start of 3rd quarter, clock 15:00, KS ball on KS35.

————— 2 plays, 2 yards, TOP 01:06 —————

Rheem, Jamie kickoff 65 yards to the OU0, touchback.

O 1-10 O20   OKLAHOMA drive start at 15:00 (3rd).

O 1-10 O20   Heupel, Josh pass incomplete to Woolfolk, Andre.

O 2-10 O20   PENALTY OU false start 5 yards to the OU15.

O 2-15 O15   Heupel, Josh pass incomplete to Fagan, Curtis.

O 3-15 O15   Heupel, Josh pass complete to Smith, Trent for 23 yards to the OU38, 1ST DOWN OU (Cooper, Jarrod;McGraw, Jon).

O 1-10 O38   Heupel, Josh pass incomplete.

O 2-10 O38   Heupel, Josh pass complete to Fagan, Curtis for 3 yards to the OU41 (Butler, J.).

O 3-7 O41   Heupel, Josh pass incomplete to Woolfolk, Andre.

O 4-7 O41   Ferguson, Jeff punt 44 yards to the KS15, Lockett, Aaron return 10 yards to the KS25, PENALTY KS illegal block 10 yards to the KS15, 1st and 10, KS ball on KS15.

————— 6 plays, 21 yards, TOP 01:50 —————

K 1-10 K15   Clock 13:10.

K 1-10 K15   Scobey, Josh rush for 3 yards to the KS18 (Williams, Roy).

K 2-7 K18   Beasley, J. rush for 5 yards to the KS23 (Klein, Kory).

K 3-2 K23   Beasley, J. rush for 10 yards to the KS33, 1ST DOWN KS (Williams, Roy).

K 1-10 K33   Beasley, J. pass incomplete to Meier, Shad.

K 2-10 K33   Beasley, J. pass complete to Lockett, Aaron for 11 yards to the KS44, 1ST

DOWN KS, out-of-bounds (Jones, Ontei).

K 1-10 K44   Beasley, J. rush for 2 yards to the KS46 (Thatcher, J.T.).

K 2-8 K46   Beasley, J. pass incomplete to Allen, David (Strait, Derrick).

K 3-8 K46   Beasley, J. pass complete to Cartwright, Rod for loss of 1 yard to the KS45 (Marshall, T.).

K 4-9 K45   Brown, Travis punt 29 yards to the OU26, Thatcher, J.T. return 5 yards to the OU31 (Kazar, Jason;Newman, Terence).

————— 8 plays, 30 yards, TOP 03:43 —————

O 1-10 O31   OKLAHOMA drive start at 09:27 (3rd).

O 1-10 O31   Heupel, Josh pass complete to Griffin,Quentin for 6 yards to the OU37 (McGraw, Jon;Cooper, Jarrod).

O 2-4 O37   Heupel, Josh pass complete to Savage, Antwone for 4 yards to the OU41, 1ST DOWN OU (Johnson, Chris).

O 1-10 O41   Griffin,Quentin rush for 5 yards to the OU46 (McGraw, Jon;Kazar, Jason).

O 2-5 O46   Heupel, Josh pass complete to Smith, Trent for 17 yards to the KS37, 1ST DOWN OU (Cooper, Jarrod).

O 1-10 K37   Heupel, Josh pass complete to Griffin,Quentin for no gain to the KS37 (Fatafehi, Mario), PENALTY KS face mask 5 yards to the KS32.

O 1-5 K32   1st and 5.

O 1-5 K32   Griffin,Quentin rush for 25 yards to the KS7, 1ST DOWN OU (Butler, J.;McGraw, Jon).

O 1-G K07   Heupel, Josh pass incomplete to Griffin,Quentin.
O 2-G K07   Heupel, Josh rush for 7 yards to the KS0, TOUCHDOWN, clock 05:54. Duncan, Tim kick attempt good.

KANSAS STATE 10, OKLAHOMA 17

————— 8 plays, 69 yards, TOP 03:33 —————

Duncan, Tim kickoff 58 yards to the KS7, Lockett, Aaron return 30 yards to the KS37 (Duncan, Tim;Wilkerson,Jimmy).
K 1-10 K37   KANSAS STATE drive start at 05:54 (3rd).
K 1-10 K37   Morgan, Quincy rush for 2 yards to the KS39 (Strait, Derrick;Callens, Corey).
K 2-8 K39   Beasley, J. pass incomplete to Lockett, Aaron.
K 3-8 K39   Beasley, J. pass incomplete to Lockett, Aaron.
K 4-8 K39   Brown, Travis punt 37 yards to the OU24, downed.
————— 3 plays, 2 yards, TOP 01:21 —————

O 1-10 O24   OKLAHOMA drive start at 04:33 (3rd).
O 1-10 O24   Heupel, Josh pass complete to Griffin,Quentin for 1 yard to the OU25 (Beisel, Monty).
O 2-9 O25   Heupel, Josh pass incomplete (Tyler, DeRon).
O 3-9 O25   Heupel, Josh pass incomplete to Woolfolk, Andre (Carter, Dyshod).
O 4-9 O25   Ferguson, Jeff punt 33 yards to the KS42, Lockett, Aaron return 58 yards to the OU0, TOUCHDOWN, clock 03:29.
————— 3 plays, 1 yards, TOP 01:04 —————

Rheem, Jamie kick attempt good.

KANSAS STATE 17, OKLAHOMA 17

Rheem, Jamie kickoff 65 yards to the OU0, Savage, Antwone return 21 yards to the OU21 (Buhl, Josh).
O 1-10 O21   OKLAHOMA drive start at 03:29 (3rd).
O 1-10 O21   Griffin,Quentin rush for 1 yard to the OU 22 (Robinson,DeVane).
O 2-9 O22   Heupel, Josh pass complete to Smith, Trent for 28 yards to the 50 yardline, 1ST DOWN OU (Cooper, Jarrod).
O 1-10 O50   Heupel, Josh sacked for loss of 10 yards to the OU40 (Leber, Ben).

O 2-20 O40   Heupel, Josh pass incomplete, PENALTY KS pass interference 12 yards to the KS48, 1ST DOWN OU, NO PLAY.

O 1-10 K48   Heupel, Josh pass complete to Griffin,Quentin for 8 yards to the KS 40 (Leber, Ben).

O 2-2 K40   Griffin,Quentin rush for 1 yard to the KS39 (Beisel, Monty).

O 3-1 K39   Heupel, Josh rush for no gain to the KS39 (Beisel, Monty).

=====END OF 3rd QUARTER=====
KANSAS STATE 17, OKLAHOMA 17

Play-by-Play Summary (4th quarter)

O 4-1 K39   Start of 4th quarter, clock 15:00.

O 4-1 K39   Griffin,Quentin rush for 22 yards to the KS17, 1ST DOWN OU (Cooper, Jarrod).

O 1-10 K17   Heupel, Josh pass complete to Woolfolk, Andre for 17 yards to the KS0,
1ST DOWN OU, TOUCHDOWN, clock 14:24.
Duncan, Tim kick attempt good.

KANSAS STATE 17, OKLAHOMA 24

---------- 9 plays, 79 yards, TOP 04:05 ----------

Duncan, Tim kickoff 60 yards to the KS5, Lockett, Aaron return 16 yards to the KS21 (Woolfolk, Andre;Everage,Brandon).

K 1-10 K21   KANSAS STATE drive start at 14:24 (4th).

K 1-10 K21   Cartwright, Rod rush for 1 yard to the KS22 (Heinecke, Corey; Holleyman, Bary).

K 2-9 K22   Scobey, Josh rush for 6 yards to the KS28 (Thatcher, J.T.).

K 3-3 K28   Beasley, J. pass incomplete to Morgan, Quincy (Thompson, M.).

K 4-3 K28   Brown, Travis punt 27 yards to the OU45, Thatcher, J.T. return 3 yards to the OU48 (Cooper, Jarrod).

---------- 3 plays, 7 yards, TOP 01:59 ----------

O 1-10 O48   OKLAHOMA drive start at 12:25 (4th).

O 1-10 O48   Heupel, Josh pass incomplete to Woolfolk, Andre.

O 2-10 O48   Heupel, Josh pass complete to Smith, Trent for 8 yards to the KS 44 (Cooper, Jarrod;Togiai, Jerry).

O 3-2 K44   Heupel, Josh pass complete to Smith, Trent for 6 yards to the KS38, 1ST

DOWN OU (Cooper, Jarrod).

O 1-10 K38   Heupel, Josh pass incomplete.

O 2-10 K38   Heupel, Josh pass complete to Fagan, Curtis for 1 yard to the KS 37 (Fatafehi, Mario).

O 3-9   K37   Heupel, Josh pass intercepted by Butler, J. at the KS29, Butler, J.

return 8 yards to the KS37 (Littrell, Seth).

————— 6 plays, 15 yards, TOP 02:11 —————

K 1-10 K37   KANSAS STATE drive start at 10:14 (4th).

K 1-10 K37   Beasley, J. pass complete to Morgan, Quincy for 25 yards to the OU38, 1ST DOWN KS, out-of-bounds.

K 1-10 O38   Beasley, J. rush for loss of 1 yard to the OU39 (Calmus, Rocky).

K 2-11 O39   Beasley, J. pass complete to Morgan, Quincy for loss of 2 yards to the OU41 (Marshall, T.).

K 3-13 O41   Beasley, J. pass incomplete to Clark, Brandon.

K 4-13 O41   Brite, Jared punt 27 yards to the OU14, out-of-bounds.

————— 4 plays, 22 yards, TOP 01:43 —————

O 1-10 O14   OKLAHOMA drive start at 08:31 (4th).

O 1-10 O14   Heupel, Josh rush for 2 yards to the OU16 (Proctor, Milton).

O 2-8   O16   Heupel, Josh pass complete to Smith, Trent for 7 yards to the OU23 (Cooper, Jarrod).

O 3-1   O23   Littrell, Seth rush for no gain to the OU23 (Beisel, Monty; Togiai, Jerry).

O 4-1   O23   Ferguson, Jeff punt 35 yards to the KS42, Allen, David return 7 yards to the KS49 (Woolfolk, Andre).

————— 3 plays, 9 yards, TOP 02:16 —————

K 1-10 K49   KANSAS STATE drive start at 06:15 (4th).

K 1-10 K49   Scobey, Josh rush for 6 yards to the OU45 (Thatcher, J.T.;Calmus, Rocky).

K 2-4   O45   Cartwright, Rod rush for no gain to the OU45 (Holleyman, Bary;Calmus, Rocky).

K 3-4   O45   Beasley, J. sacked for loss of 8 yards to the KS47 (Jones, Ontei).

K 4-12 K47   Brite, Jared punt 35 yards to the OU18, out-of-bounds.

————— 3 plays, minus 2 yards, TOP 02:11 —————

O 1-10 O18   OKLAHOMA drive start at 04:04 (4th).

O 1-10 O18   Griffin,Quentin rush for 1 yard to the OU19 (McGraw, Jon).

O 2-9   O19   Timeout Oklahoma, clock 03:12.

O 2-9   O19   Heupel, Josh rush for 8 yards to the OU27 (Tyler, DeRon;Johnson, Chris).

O 3-1 O27 Timeout Oklahoma, clock 02:37.

O 3-1 O27 Heupel, Josh rush for 3 yards to the OU30, 1ST DOWN OU (Togiai, Jerry).

O 1-10 O30 Heupel, Josh rush for 6 yards to the OU36 (Leber, Ben).

O 2-4 O36 Timeout Kansas State, clock 01:59.

O 2-4 O36 Griffin,Quentin rush for 29 yards to the KS35, 1ST DOWN OU, out-of-bounds (Leber, Ben).

O 1-10 K35 Heupel, Josh rush for 1 yard to the KS34 (Togiai, Jerry;Fatafehi, Mario).

O 2-9 K34 Timeout Kansas State, clock 01:44.

O 2-9 K34 Savage, Antwone rush for 4 yards to the KS30 (Tyler, DeRon).

O 3-5 K30 Timeout Kansas State, clock 01:35.

O 3-5 K30 Heupel, Josh rush for 2 yards to the KS28, out-of-bounds (Fatafehi, Mario).

O 4-3 K28 Timeout Oklahoma, clock 01:29.

O 4-3 K28 Duncan, Tim field goal attempt from 46 GOOD, clock 01:25.

KANSAS STATE 17, OKLAHOMA 27

————— 9 plays, 54 yards, TOP 02:39 —————

Duncan, Tim kickoff 40 yards to the KS25, Kazar, Jason return 15 yards to the KS40 (Woolfolk, Andre).

K 1-10 K40 KANSAS STATE drive start at 01:25 (4th).

K 1-10 K40 Beasley, J. pass incomplete to Wesley, Martez.

K 2-10 K40 Beasley, J. pass complete to Cartwright, Rod for 3 yards to the KS 43 (Williams, Roy).

K 3-7 K43 Beasley, J. rush for 15 yards to the OU42, 1ST DOWN KS (Klein, Kory).

K 1-10 O42 Beasley, J. pass complete to Wesley, Martez for 26 yards to the OU16, 1ST DOWN KS.

K 1-10 O16 Beasley, J. pass incomplete to Wesley, Martez.

K 2-10 O16 Beasley, J. pass complete to Morgan, Quincy for 16 yards to the OU0, 1ST DOWN KS, TOUCHDOWN, clock 00:06.

Rheem, Jamie kick attempt good.

KANSAS STATE 24, OKLAHOMA 27

————— 6 plays, 60 yards, TOP 01:19 —————

Rheem, Jamie kickoff 9 yards to the KS44, downed.
O 1-10 K44   OKLAHOMA drive start at 00:06 (4th).
O 1-10 K44   TEAM rush for loss of 2 yards to the KS46.
O 2-12 K46   End of 2nd half, clock 00:00.
————— 1 plays, minus 2 yards, TOP 00:06 —————

==========FINAL SCORE==========
KANSAS STATE 24, OKLAHOMA 27

Game 13

No. 1 OU 13, No. 2 Florida State 2

Oklahoma Rules the Nation!

MIAMI, Florida(Jan. 3, 2001) – Let the argument about who is No. 2 swirl around the country into the new year.

But there was no doubt about who is No. 1, as Oklahoma completed its perfect season by stalling the high-octane attack of No. 2 Florida State, 13-2, in the Orange Bowl.

Oklahoma did what Big 12 compatriot Nebraska couldn't do in the 1990s: beat Florida State. The biggest, toughest program on the block for the past decade couldn't score any offensive points against OU's stingy defense, settling for two charitable yet strategic points given to them by the Sooners late in the game.

"Watching Florida State, you see how athletic and talented they are, and the speed they possess," said OU quarterback Josh Heupel. "That's why Florida State is so highly touted, and the media is in awe of them. They are an extremely talented group of athletes. They're also still human."

Heisman Trophy winner Chris Weinke left the field with the single most disappointing performance of the Florida State offense in modern-era, big-game history for the school. However, Heupel, who was second in the Heisman, refused to say he felt like the National Championship Trophy had anything to do with the Heisman Trophy.

"This was never about vindication," said Heupel. "This was about Oklahoma and Florida State. I really do believe that—those aren't just words. I didn't set out to win a Heisman Trophy my senior year. That was not one of my goals. My No. 1—and only—goal was to win a national championship and a Big 12 Championship."

The Sooners were actually feeling very good about their chances going in, despite being an underdog.

"One thing Coach Stoops had to protect against was us being overconfident," Heupel said. "We were never more sure of ourselves than we were on January 3. There was never a doubt on anyone's mind that we were going to win the national championship. That confidence could be seen by everyone watching the game, whether in person or on the television."

The hype leading up to the game never rattled the Sooners, as many predicted it would.

"Our team enjoyed the entire experience," Heupel said. "The entire month of prepareation was enjoyable and exciting. This was a once-in-a-lifetime opportunity. Yet, we were business as usual getting prepared. This again goes along with what we talked about—not only enjoying the end destination, but the road to the destination as well."

That destination included a trip to the center of the media spotlight with the bid to the Orange Bowl. However, the talk changed quickly.

"It was amazing to see how the outlook of the game had changed from when the pairings for the BCS were announced to the Orange Bowl media day leading up to the game," Heupel said. "It started out as a Florida State-Oklahoma matchup, and then the debate was about whether Florida State or Miami should be in the championship game. However, on media day the question was, 'Why is the University of Oklahoma in this game playing for the national championship?'"

The hoopla was never overbearing. But it was impossible to ignore.

"The national championship game is an event all to itself,"

Heupel said. "There's so much leading up to the game that some, outside of the teams involved, forget there's a game. But that's what championship games have been blown up to be."

However, that hype leads to quite an event.

"There are not too many events during the year where there are that many people watching," Heupel said.

The Sooners became media darlings after the game.

"The tables turned so quickly with the final tick off the clock," Heupel said. "Our team was unaffected by the media, if they were praising or questioning us."

The most important step has thus been taken: OU was back. In the biggest way possible.

"It was just such a perfect ending," Heupel said. "We are now a part of Sooner tradition and excellence."

67th Annual FedEx Orange Bowl
Florida State vs Oklahoma (Jan 3, 2001 at Miami, Florida) Florida State (11-2) vs. Oklahoma (13-0)

Date: January 3, 2001 Site: Miami, Florida Stadium: Pro Player Stadium Attendance: 76,835

Score by quarters

Florida State 0	**0**	**0**	**2 - 2**	
Oklahoma 3	**0**	**3**	**7 - 13**	

Scoring summary:
First quarter

    1st 07:16 OKLAHOMA - Tim Duncan 27 yd field goal

7 plays, 44 yards, TOP 2:03, FLA-ST 0 - OKLAHOMA 3

    Third quarter

    3rd 04:24 OKLAHOMA - Tim Duncan 42 yd field goal

7 plays, 40 yards, TOP 2:09, FLA-ST 0 - OKLAHOMA 6

    Fourth quarter

    07:46 OKLAHOMA - Quentin Griffin 10 yd run (Tim Duncan kick)

2 plays, 15 yards, TOP 0:44, FLA-ST 0 - OKLAHOMA 13

    00:55 FLA-ST - Team safety, FLA-ST 2 - OKLAHOMA 13

	FSU	**OU**
First downs	14	12
Rushes-yards	17-27	36-56
Passing	274	214
Comp-Att-Int	25-52-2	25-39-1
Return Yards	21	48
Punts-Avg.	10-45	8-41
Fumbles-Lost	3-1	2-1
Penalties-Yards	6-38	7-45
Time of Possession	23:27	36:33

RUSHING: Florida St., Minor 13-20, Weinke 4-7. Oklahoma, Griffin 11-40, Heupel 13-23, Works 6-16, Littrell 2-8, Mackey 2-5, team 2-(minus 36).

PASSING: Florida St., Weinke 25-52-2-274. Oklahoma, Heupel 25-39-1-214.

RECEIVING: Florida St., Bell 7-137, Minor 5-9, Boldin 3-31, Morgan 3-21, Golightly 3-15, Walker 1-25, Gardner 1-16, Sprague 1-14, Franklin 1-6. Oklahoma, Griffin 6-23, Mackey 4-23, Works 4-3, Norman 3-49, Woolfolk 3-41, Savage 2-23, T.Smith 2-13, Fagan 1-39.

MISSED FIELD GOALS: Florida, Cimorelli 30 (WR). Oklahoma, Duncan 37 (WR).

Kickoff time: 8:24 PM End of Game: 12:01 AM Total elapsed time: 3:37
Officials: Referee: Dick Honig; Umpire: Jim Augustyn; Linesman: Jack Teitz;
Line judge: Doug Rosenbaum; Back judge: Scott Helverson;
Field judge: Henry Armstead; Side judge: Terry Anderson;
Temperature: 63 Wind: NNW 5mph Weather: Mostly cloudy

SACKS (UA-A): Florida State-Reynolds, Jamal 1-0; Warren, David 1-0; Dockett, Darnell 1-0. Oklahoma-Kory Klein.

TACKLES (UA-A): Florida State-Allen, Brian 5-7; Polley, Tommy 4-7; Thomas, Clevan 4-4; Hope, Chris 5-2; Jennings, Bradley 3-3; Gibson, Derrick 3-3; Reynolds, Jamal 2-3; Warren, David 3-1; Womble, Jeff 2-2; Samuels, Stanford 1-3; Tatum, Malcom 3-0; Cody, Tay 2-0; Brown, Rufus 2-0; Bouleware, Michael 1-0; Munyon, Matt 1-0, Jackson, Alonzo 1-0; Benford, Tony 1-0;

Dorsey, Charron 1-0; Emanual, Kevin 0-1; Dockett, Darnell 0-1; Jackson, Gennaro 0-1. Oklahoma-Thompson, Michael 5-2; Thatcher, J.T. 6-0; Marshall, Torrance 5-1; Jones Ontei 4-1; Williams, Roy 4-1; Strait, Derrick 3-0; Calmus, Rocky 3-0; Woolfolk, Andre 2-0; Wilkerson, Jimmy 2-0; Holleyman, Bary 0-2; Richardson, Ramon 0-2; Klein, Kory 1-0; Heinecke, Cory 1-0; Cody, Dan 1-0; Littrell, Seth 1-0; Everage, Brandon 0-1; Fisher, Ryan 0-1; Callens, Corey 0-1.

Play-by-Play Summary (1st quarter)
Oklahoma wins the toss and defers; Oklahoma will defend the west goal
F 1-10 F35 OKLAHOMA ball on OKLAHOMA35.
Tim Duncan kickoff 65 yards to the FLA-ST0, touchback.
F 1-10 F20 Chris Weinke pass complete to Atrews Bell for 35 yards to the OKLAHOMA 45, 1ST DOWN FLA-ST (M. Thompson).
F 1-10 O45 Travis Minor rush for 2 yards to the OKLAHOMA43 (Cory Heinecke).
F 2-8 O43 Chris Weinke pass complete to Anquan Boldin to the OKLAHOMA45, fumble forced by Ontei Jones, fumble by Anquan Boldin recovered by FLA-ST Team at OKLAHOMA 45.
F 3-10 O45 Chris Weinke pass complete to Travis Minor for 3 yards to the OKLAHOMA 42 (M.Thompson).
F 4-7 O42 Keith Cottrell punt 26 yards to the OKLAHOMA16, fair catch by J.T. Thatcher, PENALTY FLA-ST kick catching interference 6 yards to the OKLAHOMA22, 1st and 10, OKLAHOMA ball on OKLAHOMA 22.
———————— 4 plays, 38 yards, TOP 01:55 ————————
O 1-10 O22 OKLAHOMA drive start at 13:05 (1st).
O 1-10 O22 PENALTY FLA-ST offside defense 5 yards to the OKLAHOMA 27.
O 1-5 O27 Seth Littrell rush for 3 yards to the OKLAHOMA30 (Brian Allen).
O 2-2 O30 Josh Heupel sacked for loss of 6 yards to the OKLAHOMA24 (David Warren).
O 3-8 O24 Josh Heupel pass incomplete (Chris Hope).
O 4-8 O24 Jeff Ferguson punt 46 yards to the FLA-ST30, fair catch by Clevan Thomas.
———————— 3 plays, 2 yards, TOP 01:36 ————————

F 1-10 F30 FLORIDA STATE drive start at 11:29 (1st).
F 1-10 F30 FLA-ST ball on FLA-ST31.
F 1-10 F31 Travis Minor rush for 4 yards to the FLA-ST35 (J.T. Thatcher).
F 2-6 F35 Chris Weinke pass incomplete to Anquan Boldin (Cory Heinecke).
F 3-6 F35 Chris Weinke sacked for loss of 2 yards to the FLA-ST33 (Kory Klein).
F 4-8 F33 Keith Cottrell punt 51 yards to the OKLAHOMA16, J.T. Thatcher return to the OKLAHOMA26 (Brandon Moore), PENALTY FLA-ST kick catching interference off-setting, PENALTY OKLAHOMA illegal block off-setting, NO PLAY.
F 4-8 F33 Keith Cottrell punt 52 yards to the OKLAHOMA15, J.T. Thatcher return 5 yards to the OKLAHOMA20 (Rufus Brown).

————— 3 plays, 2 yards, TOP 01:48 —————

O 1-10 O20 OKLAHOMA drive start at 09:41 (1st).

O 1-10 O20 Josh Heupel pass complete to Andre Woolfolk to the OKLA-HOMA42, fumble forced by Tay Cody, fumble by Andre Woolfolk recovered by FLA-ST Clevan Thomas at OKLAHOMA47.

————— 1 plays, 27 yards, TOP 00:12 —————

F 1-10 O47 FLORIDA STATE drive start at 09:29 (1st).

F 1-10 O47 Chris Weinke pass intercepted by T. Marshall at the OKLA-HOMA34, T. Marshall return 13 yards to the OKLAHOMA47 (Charron Dorsey).

————— 1 plays, 0 yards, TOP 00:10 —————

O 1-10 O47 OKLAHOMA drive start at 09:19 (1st).

O 1-10 O47 Josh Heupel pass complete to Trent Smith for 8 yards to the FLA-ST45 (Derrick Gibson).

O 2-2 F45 Josh Heupel pass incomplete to Antwone Savage.

O 3-2 F45 Josh Heupel pass complete to Josh Norman for 36 yards to the FLA-ST9, 1ST DOWN OKLAHOMA (Derrick Gibson).

O 1-G F09 Josh Heupel pass incomplete to Josh Norman.

=====END OF 1ST QUARTER=====
FLORIDA STATE 0, OKLAHOMA 3

Play-by-Play Summary (2nd quarter)

F 1-10 F43 Start of 2nd quarter, clock 15:00.

F 1-10 F43 Travis Minor rush for 1 yard to the FLA-ST44 (Rocky Calmus).

F 2-9 F44 Travis Minor rush for 2 yards to the FLA-ST46 (Derrick Strait).

F 3-7 F46 Chris Weinke pass incomplete to Talman Gardner.

F 4-7 F46 Keith Cottrell punt 46 yards to the OKLAHOMA8, J.T. Thatcher return 10 yards to the OKLAHOMA18, fumble forced by M. Boulware, fumble by J.T. Thatcher recovered by OKLAHOMA Team at OKLAHOMA10, out-of-bounds, PENALTY OKLAHOMA personal foul 5 yards to the OKLAHOMA5, 1st and 10, OKLAHOMA ball on OKLAHOMA5.

————— 5 plays, 19 yards, TOP 01:45 —————

O 1-10 O05 OKLAHOMA drive start at 13:20 (2nd).

O 1-10 O05 Josh Heupel pass complete to Quentin Griffin for 5 yards to the OKLAHOMA10 (Jeff Womble;Derrick Gibson).

O 2-5 O10 Josh Heupel pass incomplete to Andre Woolfolk (David Warren).

O 3-5 O10 Josh Heupel pass complete to Antwone Savage for 14 yards to the OKLAHOMA24, 1ST DOWN OKLAHOMA (Clevan Thomas;Brian Allen).

O 1-10 O24 Josh Heupel pass complete to Quentin Griffin for 2 yards to the OKLAHOMA26 (Jeff Womble).

O 2-8 O26 Josh Heupel pass incomplete to Andre Woolfolk.

O 3-8 O26 Josh Heupel rush for 1 yard to the OKLAHOMA27 (Malcolm Tatum), PENALTY OKLAHOMA illegal forward pass 5 yards to the OKLA-HOMA22.

O 4-12 O22 4th and 12.

O 4-12 O22 Jeff Ferguson punt 31 yards to the FLA-ST47, Clevan Thomas return 0 yards to the FLA-ST47, fumble by Clevan Thomas recovered by FLA-ST Clevan Thomas at FLA-ST48.
———— 6 plays, 17 yards, TOP 02:20 ————

F 1-10 F48 FLORIDA STATE drive start at 11:00 (2nd).
F 1-10 F48 Chris Weinke pass complete to Randy Golightly for 8 yards to the OKLAHOMA44 (T. Marshall).
F 2-2 O44 Travis Minor rush for 3 yards to the OKLAHOMA41, 1ST DOWN FLA-ST (Jimmy Wilkerson).
F 1-10 O41 Chris Weinke pass complete to Anquan Boldin for 19 yards to the OKLAHOMA22, 1ST DOWN FLA-ST (Rocky Calmus).
F 1-10 O22 Chris Weinke pass complete to Randy Golightly for 2 yards to the OKLAHOMA20 (J.T. Thatcher).
F 2-8 O20 Timeout Oklahoma, clock 08:55.
F 2-8 O20 Chris Weinke pass complete to Travis Minor for 2 yards to the OKLAHOMA18 (Roy Williams).
F 3-6 O18 Timeout Florida State, clock 08:09.
F 3-6 O18 Chris Weinke pass complete to Travis Minor for 5 yards to the OKLAHOMA13 (Bary Holleyman;R. Richardson).
F 4-1 O13 Brett Cimorelli field goal attempt from 30 MISSED - wide right, spot at OKLAHOMA20, clock 07:30.
———— 7 plays, 40 yards, TOP 03:30 ————

O 1-10 O20 Josh Heupel pass incomplete to Andre Woolfolk.
O 2-10 O20 Josh Heupel pass complete to Josh Norman for 8 yards to the OKLAHOMA 28 (Tommy Polley;S. Samuels).
O 3-2 O28 PENALTY OKLAHOMA false start 5 yards to the OKLA-HOMA23.
O 3-7 O23 Josh Heupel pass complete to Damian Mackey for loss of 1 yard to the OKLAHOMA22 (Clevan Thomas).
O 4-8 O22 Jeff Ferguson punt 42 yards to the FLA-ST36, Clevan Thomas return 3 yards to the FLA-ST39 (Andre Woolfolk).
———— 3 plays, 2 yards, TOP 01:59 ————

=====END OF 2ND QUARTER=====
FLORIDA STATE 0, OKLAHOMA 3

Play-by-Play Summary (3rd quarter)
O 3-3 O36 Start of 3rd quarter, clock 15:00, FLA-ST ball on FLA-ST35.
———— 2 plays, 7 yards, TOP 00:49 ————

Matt Munyon kickoff 55 yards to the OKLAHOMA10, Antwone Savage return 36 yards to the OKLAHOMA46, out-of-bounds (Matt Munyon).
O 1-10 O46 OKLAHOMA drive start at 15:00 (3rd).
O 1-10 O46 Josh Heupel pass complete to Renaldo Works for no gain to the OKLAHOMA46 (Clevan Thomas).
O 2-10 O46 Josh Heupel rush for 7 yards to the FLA-ST47 (Chris Hope).

O 3-3 F47 Josh Heupel pass complete to Andre Woolfolk for 7 yards to the FLA-ST40, 1ST DOWN OKLAHOMA (Malcolm Tatum).

O 1-10 F40 Quentin Griffin rush for 6 yards to the FLA-ST34 (Tommy Polley;Brian Allen).

O 2-4 F34 PENALTY OKLAHOMA false start 5 yards to the FLA-ST39.

O 2-9 F39 Josh Heupel pass complete to Andre Woolfolk for 7 yards to the FLA-ST32 (Malcolm Tatum).

O 3-2 F32 Josh Heupel pass complete to Renaldo Works for 2 yards to the FLA-ST30, 1ST DOWN OKLAHOMA, out-of-bounds (Clevan Thomas).

O 1-10 F30 Renaldo Works rush for 7 yards to the FLA-ST23 (Derrick Gibson;S. Samuels).

O 2-3 F23 Renaldo Works rush for 2 yards to the FLA-ST21 (Tommy Polley;Brian Allen).

O 3-1 F21 Renaldo Works rush for 2 yards to the FLA-ST19, 1ST DOWN OKLAHOMA (Brian Allen).

O 1-10 F19 PENALTY OKLAHOMA false start 5 yards to the FLA-ST24.

O 1-15 F24 Josh Heupel pass complete to Damian Mackey for 8 yards to the FLA-ST16 (Tommy Polley).

O 2-7 F16 Josh Heupel pass complete to Quentin Griffin for loss of 4 yards to the FLA-ST20 (Tommy Polley).

O 3-11 F20 Josh Heupel pass incomplete to Quentin Griffin.

O 4-11 F20 Tim Duncan field goal attempt from 37 MISSED - wide right, spot at FLA-ST20, clock 08:01.
————— 13 plays, 34 yards, TOP 06:59 —————

F 1-10 F20 Chris Weinke pass complete to Nick Franklin for 6 yards to the FLA-ST26 (Derrick Strait).

F 2-4 F26 Travis Minor rush for loss of 1 yard to the FLA-ST25 (Roy Williams).

F 3-5 F25 Chris Weinke pass incomplete to Atrews Bell.

F 4-5 F25 Keith Cottrell punt 41 yards to the OKLAHOMA34, fair catch by J.T. Thatcher.
————— 3 plays, 5 yards, TOP 01:28 —————

O 1-10 O34 OKLAHOMA drive start at 06:33 (3rd).

O 1-10 O34 OKLAHOMA ball on OKLAHOMA35.

O 1-10 O35 Josh Heupel pass incomplete to Trent Smith.

O 2-10 O35 Josh Heupel rush for 1 yard to the OKLAHOMA36 (Tony Benford).

O 3-9 O36 Josh Heupel pass complete to Curtis Fagan for 39 yards to the FLA-ST25, 1ST DOWN OKLAHOMA (Chris Hope).

O 1-10 F25 Josh Heupel pass incomplete to Antwone Savage.

O 2-10 F25 Quentin Griffin rush for no gain to the FLA-ST25 (David Warren).

O 3-10 F25 Josh Heupel pass incomplete to Seth Littrell, dropped pass.

O 4-10 F25 Tim Duncan field goal attempt from 42 GOOD, clock 04:24.

=====END OF 3RD QUARTER=====
FLORIDA STATE 0, OKLAHOMA 6

Play-by-Play Summary (4th quarter)

O 2-2 F45 Start of 4th quarter, clock 15:00.

O 2-2 F45 Josh Heupel rush for 1 yard to the FLA-ST44 (Chris Hope).

O 3-1 F44 Renaldo Works rush for no gain to the FLA-ST44 (Jamal Reynolds).

O 4-1 F44 Jeff Ferguson punt 26 yards to the FLA-ST18, out-of-bounds.

———— 4 plays, 9 yards, TOP 01:51 ————

F 1-10 F18 FLORIDA STATE drive start at 13:31 (4th).

F 1-10 F18 FLA-ST ball on FLA-ST19.

F 1-10 F19 Chris Weinke pass complete to Robert Morgan for 16 yards to the FLA-ST35, 1ST DOWN FLA-ST, out-of-bounds (M. Thompson).

F 1-10 F35 Chris Weinke pass complete to Robert Morgan for 1 yard to the FLA-ST36 (M. Thompson).

F 2-9 F36 Chris Weinke pass incomplete to Atrews Bell, PENALTY OKLA-HOMA pass interference 15 yards to the OKLAHOMA49, 1ST DOWN FLA-ST, NO PLAY.

F 1-10 O49 Chris Weinke pass complete to Ryan Sprague for 14 yards to the OKLAHOMA35, 1ST DOWN FLA-ST, out-of-bounds (M. Thompson).

F 1-10 O35 Chris Weinke pass incomplete to Anquan Boldin.

F 2-10 O35 Chris Weinke pass incomplete to Robert Morgan.

F 3-10 O35 Chris Weinke pass incomplete to Atrews Bell (Brandon Everage).

F 4-10 O35 Timeout Florida State, clock 12:14.

F 4-10 O35 Chris Weinke pass incomplete to Anquan Boldin (Derrick Strait).

———— 8 plays, 46 yards, TOP 01:24 ————

O 1-10 O35 OKLAHOMA drive start at 12:07 (4th).

O 1-10 O35 Josh Heupel rush for 7 yards to the OKLAHOMA42 (Chris Hope).

O 2-3 O42 Josh Heupel pass complete to Quentin Griffin for 4 yards to the OKLAHOMA46, 1ST DOWN OKLAHOMA (Clevan Thomas;Brian Allen).

O 1-10 O46 Josh Heupel pass complete to Josh Norman for 5 yards to the FLA-ST49 (Brian Allen;Tommy Polley).

O 2-5 F49 Josh Heupel pass complete to Renaldo Works for 4 yards to the FLA-ST45 (Clevan Thomas;S. Samuels).

O 3-1 F45 Josh Heupel pass incomplete to Josh Norman.

O 4-1 F45 Jeff Ferguson punt 40 yards to the FLA-ST5, downed.

———— 5 plays, 20 yards, TOP 02:48 ————

F 1-10 F05 FLORIDA STATE drive start at 09:19 (4th).

F 1-10 F05 FLA-ST ball on FLA-ST6.

F 1-10 F06 Timeout Oklahoma, clock 09:19.

F 1-10 F06 Chris Weinke pass complete to Robert Morgan for 4 yards to the FLA-ST10 (J.T. Thatcher).

F 2-6 F10 Chris Weinke pass incomplete to Robert Morgan.

F 3-6 F10 Chris Weinke rush to the FLA-ST15, fumble forced by Rocky Calmus, fumble by Chris Weinke recovered by OKLAHOMA Roy Williams at FLA-ST17, Roy Williams for 2 yards to the FLA-ST15.
————— 3 plays, 11 yards, TOP 00:49 —————

O 1-10 F15 OKLAHOMA drive start at 08:30 (4th), OKLAHOMA ball on FLA-ST15.
O 1-10 F15 Josh Heupel rush for 5 yards to the FLA-ST10 (David Warren; Derrick Gibson).
O 2-5 F10 Quentin Griffin rush for 10 yards to the FLA-ST0, 1ST DOWN OKLAHOMA, TOUCHDOWN, clock 07:46.
O 1-G F03 PENALTY OKLAHOMA substitution infraction 5 yards to the FLA-ST8.
Tim Duncan kick attempt good.

FLORIDA STATE 2, OKLAHOMA 13

————— 2 plays, 15 yards, TOP 00:44 —————
Tim Duncan kickoff 65 yards to the FLA-ST0, touchback.
F 1-10 F20 FLORIDA STATE drive start at 07:46 (4th).
F 1-10 F20 Chris Weinke pass incomplete to Javon Walker (J.T. Thatcher).
F 2-10 F20 Chris Weinke pass complete to Atrews Bell for 43 yards to the OKLAHOMA37, 1ST DOWN FLA-ST.
F 1-10 O37 Chris Weinke pass incomplete to Atrews Bell.
F 2-10 O37 Travis Minor rush for loss of 3 yards to the OKLAHOMA40 (J.T. Thatcher).
F 3-13 O40 Chris Weinke pass incomplete to Anquan Boldin.
F 4-13 O40 Chris Weinke pass incomplete to Travis Minor.
————— 6 plays, 40 yards, TOP 01:25 —————

O 1-10 O40 OKLAHOMA drive start at 06:21 (4th).
O 1-10 O40 Josh Heupel rush for 1 yard to the OKLAHOMA41 (Brian Allen).
O 2-9 O41 Damian Mackey rush for 5 yards to the OKLAHOMA46 (Clevan Thomas).
O 3-4 O46 Josh Heupel sacked for loss of 7 yards to the OKLAHOMA39 (Jamal Reynolds;Darnell Dockett).
O 4-11 O39 Jeff Ferguson punt 42 yards to the FLA-ST19, Clevan Thomas return 1 yard to the FLA-ST20, out-of-bounds (Ontei Jones).
————— 3 plays, minus 1 yards, TOP 02:35 —————

F 1-10 F20 FLORIDA STATE drive start at 03:46 (4th).
F 1-10 F20 Chris Weinke pass incomplete (Jimmy Wilkerson).
F 2-10 F20 Chris Weinke pass complete to Atrews Bell for no gain to the FLA-ST20 (Derrick Strait).
F 3-10 F20 Chris Weinke pass complete to Travis Minor for loss of 5 yards to the FLA-ST15 (T. Marshall).
F 4-15 F15 Keith Cottrell punt 58 yards to the OKLAHOMA27, downed.
————— 3 plays, minus 5 yards, TOP 01:38 —————

O 1-10 O27 OKLAHOMA drive start at 02:08 (4th).

O 1-10 O27 Quentin Griffin rush for 3 yards to the OKLAHOMA30 (David-Warren).

O 2-7 O30 Josh Heupel rush for 5 yards to the OKLAHOMA35 (Chris Hope).

O 3-2 O35 Timeout Florida State, clock 01:52.

O 3-2 O35 Renaldo Works rush for no gain to the OKLAHOMA35 (Jeff Womble; Jamal Reynolds).

O 4-2 O35 Team rush for loss of 35 yards to the OKLAHOMA0 (S. Samuels), Team safety, clock 00:55.

FLORIDA STATE 2, OKLAHOMA 13

————— 4 plays, minus 27 yards, TOP 01:13 —————

Jeff Ferguson kickoff 64 yards to the FLA-ST16, out-of-bounds, FLA-ST ball on FLA-ST17.

F 1-10 F17 FLORIDA STATE drive start at 00:54 (4th).

F 1-10 F17 Chris Weinke pass complete to Javon Walker for 25 yards to the FLA-ST42, 1ST DOWN FLA-ST, out-of-bounds (J.T. Thatcher).

F 1-10 F42 Chris Weinke pass complete to Anquan Boldin for 14 yards to the OKLAHOMA44, 1ST DOWN FLA-ST (Roy Williams).

F 1-10 O44 Chris Weinke pass incomplete to Anquan Boldin.

F 2-10 O44 Chris Weinke pass complete to Atrews Bell for 14 yards to the OKLAHOMA30, 1ST DOWN FLA-ST (M. Thompson;Brandon Everage).

F 1-10 O30 Team pass incomplete.

F 2-10 O30 Chris Weinke pass intercepted by Ontei Jones at the OKLAHOMA 0,Ontei Jones return 0 yards to the OKLAHOMA0, touchback.

————— 6 plays, 53 yards, TOP 00:38 —————

OKLAHOMA drive start at 00:16 (4th).

O 1-10 O20 Team rush for loss of 1 yard to the OKLAHOMA19.

O 2-11 O19 End of 2nd half, clock 00:00.

————— 1 play, minus 1 yard, TOP 00:16 —————

=======FINAL SCORE=======
FLORIDA STATE 2, OKLAHOMA 13

ABOUT THE AUTHOR
BOB SCHALLER

Bob Schaller has more than 20 books in print, including the widely popular children's series, X-Country Adventures from Baker Book House, which includes the titles *South Dakota Treaty Search, Adventure in Wyoming, Crime in a Colorado Cave and Message in Montana, Treasure in Texas* and *Mystery in Massachusetts.* His other work includes *For God and Country: Foundations of Faith* with Air Force Academy Football Coach Fisher DeBerry and *The Adventures of Jack and Diane, Volume I* a Christian children's sports series. Bob Schaller can be reached at schallerrc@aol.com.